D1108486

THE EDUCATIONAL MISSION OF THE CHURCH

THE EDUCATIONAL MISSION OF THE CHURCH

by

ROBERT J. HAVIGHURST

Philadelphia
THE WESTMINSTER PRESS

LIBRARY OF CONGRESS CATALOG CARD No. 65-10538

PUBLISHED BY THE WESTMINSTER PRESS®

PHILADELPHIA, PENNSYLVANIA

PRINTED IN THE UNITED STATES OF AMERICA

To the memory of my father
The Rev. Freeman A. Havighurst
1869–1961

CONTENTS

INTRODUCTION

The writer is a liberal Christian. His grandfather was a German Methodist immigrant and minister, who founded the German Wallace College in Iowa, which was later joined to the Iowa Wesleyan College. In the following generation, three of the five sons went into the Methodist ministry, including the writer's father.

During the writer's own lifetime, he has seen The Methodist Church evolve from a rural-based, testimonial-giving, revival-oriented group to a liberal, world-minded church that is coping with the ethical problem of racial integration. He is now a member of a Baptist–United Church congregation, where at one time he served as principal of the high school department of the church school. He has been a consultant on education to the National Council of Churches, was formerly a member of the Advisory Committee on Research in Religious Education for the National Council, and is currently a member of the Research Committee of the Religious Education Association.

For the writer, the church is a favorite object of study within his field of special interest, which is the social psychology of human development and human behavior. The church is also a rich source of boyhood associations. He learned to see the local community and the wide world through the eyes of the church at a time when the public school had a narrow vision and a limited horizon. The church helped to free and to extend his mind. He learned to ask questions about the ethics of society. Beulah Land was a part of his geography — self-taught and reaching out beyond the school geography. Martin Luther's life he read at the age of ten from a history of the Reformation in his father's library, and he had to conclude from internal evidence that the Diet of Worms was not an alimentary event.

This book deals with religious education as seen by a social scientist. It attempts to explore and explain the educational functions of churches in a society where:

Responsibilities of state and church for education are separated;
The society has become urbanized and industrialized;
The whole world is becoming economically and politically interdependent;
The authority of the church on secular matters is questioned by many people;
Many churches do not assert a claim to authority on secular matters;
Belief in the supernatural is decreasing;
Ecumenism is growing;
Churches are analyzing their social functions and responsibilities in the midst of severe social crises.

The suggestions in this book for the content of religious education are made with the purpose of showing how social science may be instrumental for the achievement of goals set by religious thinkers and writers. As a social scientist, the writer would not presume to state goals for religious education. He has accepted the goals as defined by religious educators and he has attempted, as a social scientist, to present ideas about content and method of religious education that may help religious educators to achieve these goals in the contemporary world.

The writer wishes to express his thanks and his appreciation to the faculty of Princeton Theological Seminary for the opportunity to give the L. P. Stone Lectures in 1964, which form the core of this book.

R. J. H.

Chicago, Illinois

I. THE CHURCH AS AN EDUCATIVE INSTITUTION: WHAT AND HOW IT TEACHES

Every church recognizes that it must teach. It must teach its children and young people and its converts. At the same time it must teach its adult members, since the lessons of religion cannot all be learned by children. Most of its teaching is informal; some of it is formal.

What the Church Teaches

The church teaches knowledge, habits, attitudes, and beliefs.

Knowledge. The church teaches knowledge from and concerning its Holy Book; the history of the church; the present activities of the church in other places; and its theology.

Habits. The church teaches certain religious habits and practices, such as prayer, communion, confession, liturgy, hymns, and the habit of church attendance. The church also teaches moral habits and avoidance of those habits it considers immoral.

Attitudes. Every church teaches attitudes of loyalty to the local church and to its denomination. It also teaches social-civic attitudes that it regards as productive of a wholesome and religiously oriented society. It teaches a world view — a set of attitudes about other nations, other peoples, other churches, and about the nature and goals of world history.

Beliefs. A church teaches a set of beliefs about the supernatural, a code of ethics, and beliefs about the proper relationship between man and God.

The teaching of a church is always related to the *social condition* of the people it serves. Even though they share a heritage of religious tradition and a set of Holy Scriptures, the members of a given church in two different countries will learn differently from their common heritage. And two specific churches that serve different social classes will teach differently because they teach people with a social class difference. Thus a Methodist church in a prosperous suburb will teach differently from a Methodist church in a rural village, and differently again from a Methodist church in a working-class section of a big city. To some extent a church consists of people teaching themselves, and if the people of two different churches are quite different, the churches will teach differently.

The teaching of the Jewish church changed drastically when the Jewish people emerged from the ghettos of Europe. In the ghetto situation the church taught so as to make religious and social life serve the needs of the people in a society that was crowded together, hemmed in, and under constant and pitiless pressure from outside. This teaching was no longer relevant when the Jews were able to spread out in Europe, and to emigrate to America.

This relation of the church teaching to its social situation is closer in a society where there is no state church. A state church tends to have a common teaching for all its members, though it often fails to reach large numbers of its nominal members.

When a society or a group within a society is undergoing rapid social change, its religious teaching is likely to be changing. Thus today, in the rapidly changing contemporary society, the churches are changing their teaching. One sees this in reading the papal encyclicals of the Roman Catholic Church in the present century. Another set of changes of almost revolutionary proportions is taking place in the Negro Protestant churches of the United States, related to the assumption of social and political power by Negroes.

History of the Church as Educator

In theocratic societies, where the state government and the state religion are very closely related, the church has a monopoly of formal education. Europe in the Middle Ages was such a society, and then the church spoke with authority on what people should believe and how they should live, because the claim of the church to know these matters was generally accepted. Then the national state arose to take over some of the functions earlier performed by the universal church. The state became the source of morality, mutual political and military cooperation, and, indeed, of human brotherhood within a restricted sphere.

The national state then became the teacher of the people, and the church had either to go into partnership with the state or to restrict its educational scope to areas left open by the state. If there had been only one church after the rise of national states, this one church might have become the state church and might have continued its educational leadership. But coexistence of Protestants and Catholics in the same states, and the fragmentation of Protestantism, led to separation of church and state in many countries, with the state taking responsibility for most of formal education. On the other hand, the Reformation demanded a more active and explicit form of religious education within the Protestant churches. People must be taught to read and to understand the Bible.

The rise of the national state to political and economic power without religious sanction or religious control has created times and situations in which the church was in conflict with the state. Again and again, during the recent centuries and decades, representatives of the church have warned and counseled the government on political matters because the state proposed to go against the teaching and the mission of the church. Today the church often stands for moral laws that are flouted by the governments. Thus there are national governments today that support forms of warfare, racial intolerance and discrimination, economic discrimination and injustice, that some or all of the churches cannot support and, in fact, actually teach against.

Thus the churches of the majority of countries today teach in the moral and religious spheres independent of the state and sometimes in opposition to the state. At the same time, the various churches differ a good deal and are sometimes in conflict over their moral and religious teaching.

Churches generally recognize the power and the right of the state to control education in the areas of political and economic instruction.

With the national state in charge of nonreligious education in most countries, the church is restricted to the educational areas mentioned above — to teaching knowledge, habits, attitudes, and beliefs that have a religious nature or a religious sanction. These are the explicit educational functions of the church, but one cannot deny that the church has a powerful educative influence outside these areas.

The church is not always in conflict with society on moral issues. More often than not, the church is the institution that promotes morality as it is defined by the state. But in a complex modern state there are likely to be various versions of public morality, and the various churches may espouse or perhaps give rise to these various versions.

Effectiveness of Church Teaching

The view that the church has a considerable influence on human behavior is based on the following two propositions, which have grown out of the school of sociology to which Max Weber was a principal contributor.

1. Every religious group develops its own distinctive orientation toward all aspects of life.

2. The religious orientation of a group is fairly independent of the social situation (social class, socioeconomic status) of the group.

This opinion is not very popular among American sociologists, who generally believe that urbanism and industrialization have promoted secularism in the twentieth century and thus tended to reduce differences of attitude and orientation between religions.

However, Gerhard Lenski has found partial support for these propositions in a study of social and religious attitudes and beliefs in Detroit.[1] His procedure was to compare the differences between socioeconomic groups with the differences between four religious groups: Roman Catholic, Jewish, White Protestant, and Negro Protestant. Lenski found that differences between the four socioreligious groups when social class was controlled were about the same size as the differences between social classes when religious group was controlled. Religious differences were greater than social class differences on attitudes toward gambling, drinking, dancing, birth control, and Sunday closing of business. Social class differences were greater than religious differences on preferences for the use of leisure time. Religious differences were greater than social class differences in "present versus future orientation," with the Protestants more than the Catholics favoring the postponement of present pleasures for the sake of greater future rewards.

These findings suggest a rather strong relationship between religion and general social attitudes, and, since most of the people were born into their religion, the conclusion might well be that religion had an educative influence upon these attitudes, acting probably through the family.

Admitting that the church has less power over the lives of people than it had a few centuries ago, nevertheless it is true that the church has greater influence on the social attitudes of people than has any other major social institution except the family.

How the Church Teaches

The process by which the church teaches is better called *socialization* than *instruction*. The church is one of the agencies that makes the human infant into a social being. Operating directly on the individual as well as through his family, the church enlists his time and his emotional involvement in church activities. The entire church life is a teaching program, just as family life is a teaching program. This has been stated by D. Campbell Wyckoff as follows:

Where does Christian education take place? Fundamentally, it takes place in the worshiping and witnessing community of persons in Christ. This community has a life, a message, a mission, and a heritage. It has been brought into being, sustained, and directed by God to continue his reconciling work in Jesus Christ. The gospel is its message; the Holy Spirit is its power; love is its mood. The life it lives and the work it does are as varied as the expressions it finds in the home, the school, the neighborhood, the congregational life and worship, the missionary enterprise, Christian service and social action, and all the ways in which the ecumenical spirit is brought to reality. Christian education in this context becomes nurture in the fellowship of love.[2]

Explicit instruction is a small part of religious education, though it should not be a minor part. With some churches the explicit instruction tends to be concentrated at certain critical points in the life cycle, such as confirmation at the beginning of adolescence, marital instruction just before marriage, instruction concerning the religious upbringing of children when there are young children in the home. With other churches, there is a regular program of explicit instruction during childhood and youth.

The need for *formal instruction* is different in different religious groups. Historically, the coming of the Protestant Reformation created a demand for universal Christian education among Protestants. Reading the Bible was urged on the common people because of the doctrine that a true believer must *understand his faith*. He was expected to understand the Word of God and to respond to it with religious faith. To facilitate this kind of religious education, the Bible was translated into the vernacular, family Bible-reading and prayer were urged, and Christian schools were established where Lutheranism and Calvinism were strong.

The Jews had their reasons also for formal instruction in Hebrew and in reading the Jewish scriptures.

The development of state-supported primary schools in northern Europe after the fragmentation of Protestantism made it difficult if not impossible to give religious instruction in the state schools, since the various Protestant denominations did not agree on a common religious curriculum. Although the growing religious tolerance of the twentieth century has allowed state-supported schools to give religious instruction and even to be controlled by religious groups in several countries (especially Holland, Germany, and England), the religious denominations or sects with a pietistic leaning have tended to mistrust religious instruction that was not clearly controlled by them. For example, it seems that some Dutch pietistic groups prefer not to send their children to state-supported schools where Protestant religious instruction is given. Rather, they choose to send their children to public schools without religious instruction, and then to give religious instruction in their own way.

In the United States, the churches at first made no attempt to use the state schools for religious instruction. One alternative was a system of parochial schools, but this was not popular among the Protestants. The Presbyterians tried this out, with some 260 parochial schools established in the period around 1850, but most of these were abandoned by 1870. Most Protestant churches turned to the Sunday school.

The period from 1850 to 1890 was the heyday of the Sunday school movement in the United States. Some denominations joined together for planning the curriculum, and the American Sunday School Union adopted the Uniform Lesson Plan in 1872. The decades before 1900 also saw the development of young people's societies in Protestant churches, such as the Epworth League, Christian Endeavor, and the Baptist Young Peoples Union.

Formal Versus Informal Methods. We have had a century of formal religious education in Protestant churches. During this time the Sunday school has become established, church youth organizations, vacation Bible classes, church camps and institutes, have come, and religious educational work has become a profession. The teachers or practitioners of formal religious education are directors of religious education, church school teachers and youth group leaders, priests, pastors, and rabbis.

In addition to groups organized by the church for educational purposes, there are four other media of education, none of them explicitly educational but all with educational value. They are:

1. *The Small Group.* A young married couples club, a club of working women, a club of old people, a college students club, a Bible study group, etc. These groups exist for fellowship purposes, and only a few of them have the purpose of studying. But they are likely to influence the attitudes and beliefs and moral habits of their members.

2. *The Sermon.* The sermon is aimed to help promote spiritual growth, and in so doing, it often conveys knowledge and stimulates beliefs and attitudes.

3. *The Liturgy.* With its poetic language, color, light, and movement, the liturgy teaches reverence and builds loyalty to the church.

4. *Pastoral Consultation or Counseling.* Whether in the form of counseling or through confession the church member seeks a kind of spiritual as well as moral enlightenment.

Other informal educational influences of the church appear in participation in a variety of religious activities. For example, the child who brings a gift for the poor at Thanksgiving time may be learning charity.

Then the church educates informally and indirectly through its advice to parents on the religious rearing of children, and in this way through family religious and moral teaching.

The Case of Roberta. To weigh the relative effectiveness of formal and informal educational procedures, it is useful to look at individuals who have grown up in the church and to analyze their religious experience in educational terms. Roberta was one of a group who grew up in Prairie City and were studied over a period of ten years, from age ten to age twenty. She was one of the outstanding all-round students and persons in her group.[3] Born to an average couple of lower-middle-class status, she had an orderly and affectionate home experience. Far more talented and intelligent than her parents, she found in them a stable basis for her character and personality development. They were hardly more than nominal church members, and kept separate memberships in two Protestant churches. Roberta attended her mother's church, starting Sunday school at an early age and attending regularly until she reached her teens, but she was never as active and outstanding in her church as she was in school. There she was one of those who took responsibility for leadership as early as the seventh grade, and her musical and artistic talents made her much in demand for school music groups as well as for committee work on school parties. When judged by a research group of psychologists, she was given ratings at the top of her class on the qualities of " Strength of Conscience and Scale of Values " and " Getting Along with Age-Mates."

When she was sixteen she took a Sunday school class of five-year-olds, and built up the attendance from eight children to twelve. She liked children, and her artistic ability enabled her to prepare attractive materials for them to work with on Sunday mornings. Although she was encouraged by her teachers to take a course in art after graduating from high school, she decided to stay at home, where she took a secretarial job during the year that she waited before marrying a boy who had a year of college and then came back home to work. Now, at about thirty, he is working for an insurance company and Roberta has three children. She expects to become active in church work in another few years, when her children are older.

Family, school, and church seem to have cooperated smoothly, informally, and unconsciously to make Roberta into an attractive and competent person. Formal religious education seems to have played little or no part in her ethical and religious development. But one is tempted to ask whether she would not have become a more influential and effective person in her church and her community if she had been given more intellectual stimulation in school and church and if she had been challenged by a deeper understanding of the mission of the church in the modern world.

Comparison of Church with Secular Education. Clearly, the church relies more on informal education than the secular school does. The church gives some instruction, and provides the setting for experiences in applying religious attitudes and beliefs to the neighborhood and local and wider community. The school gives much more instruction and often provides experience in applying wholesome social attitudes to the problems of society.

In addition, the church does something important that few secular schools are able to do. The church provides *nurture,* through involving the individual in the atmosphere and relationships of the church fellowship. It is more than a hundred years since Horace Bushnell wrote on *Christian Nurture*. His statements seem profoundly true today.

> This is the very idea of Christian education, that it begins with nurture, or cultivation. . . . It is the only true idea of Christian education that the child is to grow up in the life of the parent and be a Christian in principle from its earliest years. . . . No truth is really taught by words, or interpreted by intellectual and logical methods; truth must be lived into meaning, before it can be truly known.[4]

Another difference between the church and the secular school program is that the church program is explicitly concerned with attitudes, beliefs, and ethical behavior, while the secular school has a wide range of objectives related on the one hand to the intellectual development of the individual and on the other hand to preparing the student for economic, civic, and social roles in the society.

Finally, participation in the church program is voluntary, whereas the secular school program is compulsory up to mid-adolescence. This means that the church has little or no influence on a substantial proportion of the population. In two Midwestern communities that the writer has studied, the proportions of youth who were unknown to any clergymen were 30 and 40 percent. Probably even less of the youth in a big city have contact with a church.

Affective Versus Intellective Education

The preceding discussion of informal versus formal education is an introduction to a basic distinction that will now be made and will be carried through the other sections of this book — the distinction between *affective* and *intellective* education.

Affective education and affective learning are teaching and learning in which feelings and emotions are predominant. In such education there is an explicit aim to develop emotional and moral sensitivities, and whatever factual knowledge results has minor significance. The passions are involved in affective education. In affective education, values have a priority. The making of value judgments is encouraged. The child who experiences the Catholic Mass as a thing of color and movement and music and incense, all combining to stimulate and please his senses, is being taught affectively to love the church. The girl who is taught that she can take her sorrows and her aspirations in prayer to Mary, Our Lady of Sorrows, is being educated affectively. The Protestant boy who experiences the melodious and simple rhythms of the gospel song about "Beulah Land" and has visions when he sings,

> I look away across the sea
> Where mansions are prepared for me

is getting an affective experience that binds him to the literal theology of his church. The low-church Episcopalian who is brought up in the liturgy of that church comes to prefer it to the "barren" Methodist service and yet to dislike the "popish" liturgy of the high church. This is all affective education.

Affective religious education also may include didactic teaching about the evils of dancing or card-playing or having music in the church, as well as the virtues of meditation on Sunday, of tithing, and of "turning the other cheek."

Affective education employs the arts and literature and other nonrational products of man rather than science and logic and the other human products that require factual knowledge and rational analysis.

Affective education is not necessarily anti-intellectual. In fact, literary and aesthetic criticism are highly intellectual activities carried on with respect to the affective side of life. But affective education minimizes rational analysis and maximizes value judgments, moral judgments, and the development of positive and negative attitudes based on learning experiences which do not contain reflective thinking.

During the European Middle Ages, the Roman Catholic Church enjoyed a quasi-universal acceptance of its view of the nature of man, of God, and of history. The church then translated the basic conception into a number of different forms, some affective and some intellective. There were church frescoes and cathedral carvings, special local saints, and a repertory of morality plays that were repeated year after year with the approval and enjoyment of the common people, much as young children want a familiar story read over and over. At the same time there was an intellectual version for those to whom intellective education was given, which contained the sophisticated theological and philosophical discussions of the Schoolmen. Toynbee writes of theology as "the price a religion pays for conversion of intellectuals." Equally, one might say, myths and parables and morality plays and holy pictures are the price a religion pays for the conversion of common people in a simple society.

Intellective education is teaching and learning in which rational analysis predominates. Religious conviction and religious faith are used as foundations for intellective religious education, but the structure built on them is logical and has empirical validity. The twentieth-century inquiry into foreign missions is an example of the move from affective to intellective in the life of the church. Church people asked themselves, "What should foreign missions accomplish, and are we achieving what we want through foreign missions?" They asked themselves what it meant to save a soul by conversion to Christianity. They asked themselves what was the meaning of Christian discipleship in countries where hunger and poverty and disease were the rule among the mass of people, or where the society was torn by blood feuds. Thus they learned intellectively to look critically at foreign missions, and they proceeded to reform the mission movement.

The inexorable drive toward intellective education in secular life was a result of the development of science and technology in the modern world. As secular was separated from religious education, the education supported by the state became more and more intellective. Perhaps it has become too much intellective, as some of the literary and artistic humanists of this century warn us when they attempt to restore affective education to some of its earlier preeminence in secular education.

Intellective education in the public schools is becoming promoted and bettered today in much of the new teaching that aims to make the mind an instrument for learning, and attempts to teach children to "think like" mathematicians, scientists, and other specialists of a technological society. One of the more significant areas of experimental education is that of "education for inquiry" which aims to teach elementary school youngsters to inquire into physical and social phenomena as physical and social scientists do.

The movement toward intellective teaching is not so striking in religious education, but in the judgment of this writer it is a fundamental movement for bringing the Kingdom of God to a modern, complex, urban, industrial, and interdependent world. The papal encyclicals of this century call Roman Catholics to understand the social world and to take intellectually sound steps in keeping with their religious ideals. The increasing this-worldliness of the leading churches and churchmen forces them to employ intellective as well as affective education with the men and women and children who make up their churches.

If the church is to exert a religious influence on the metropolitan problems of the big city conglomerates or on the international problems of war and peace and foreign aid, the people of the church must have more than naïve charity to guide their actions. Church education must be increasingly intellective. The trend in this direction is seen clearly if one analyzes the forms and content of religious education over the past century.

It must be admitted, however, that the movement to reduce the affective and increase the intellective in religious education is a middle-class movement. It does not show in churches with a lower-class membership. Often this is the cause of mistrust and and ill will between churches with different emphasis, or between congregations within the same church denomination which differ in their social class compositions.

A major problem for religious education in this decade is to combine intellective with affective education in such ways that they interact with and mutually support each other. They are not necessarily or inevitably opposed, but they often appear to be opposed when one or the other is wrongly used. Incidentally, this is also a major problem for secular education.

The affective-intellective combination that the Roman Catholic Church worked out for the Middle Ages may have been good for its day, but clearly nothing like it will do for the present situation. We need a synthesis fitting to the second half of the twentieth century.

Needed — A New Synthesis

During the past hundred years, religious education in a formal sense has come into existence and is now a complex phenomenon, with various forms in various churches. It might be said that these hundred years have seen a search for a new synthesis of affective and intellective religious education, and that the search is by no means ended.

Rise of the Religious Education Movement. During the nineteenth century the great majority of Protestant churches in the United States decided to carry on the religious education of their youth through a Sunday educational program. They ruled out the public schools because of the principle of separation of church and state, combined with their distrust of one another as sources of correct teaching. Most of the Protestant churches ruled out the parochial school as an answer. And they decided that the family alone was not adequate for the religious education of children, though they relied on the family to bring or send the children to church school, to hold family prayer, and in general to support the efforts of the church. It appears that the Protestant churches generally underestimated the importance of the family in the religious education of children.

The Sunday school movement reached its peak about 1900, and the Protestant churches generally had Sunday afternoon and evening youth meetings in addition to the morning Sunday school. Around the beginning of the twentieth century, there began the professionalization of religious education. The leading Protestant churches had resources for what was clearly a development of major importance to them. The conviction was growing that religious education needed more systematic study and thought and more organization. It needed a philosophy, a procedure for training volunteer teachers, a curriculum. In 1903 the Religious Education Association was established, and the profession of religious educator came into existence as distinct from that of clergyman. The International Council of Religious Education was formed in 1922, with a merger of the International Sunday School Association and the Sunday School Council of Evangelical Denominations.

By the 1920's the *scientific-pedagogical* approach to religious education was well established, and was growing in parallel with the developing pedagogy of secular education and was considerably influenced by it. The graded curriculum was being developed by several denominations. The content of the curriculum was no longer entirely Biblical. Besides the Bible, there was material on the history of the church, on comparative religions, on foreign missions, and on the socioethical problems of contemporary society.

In addition to the Sunday school, the churches were developing a range of educational activities—the vacation Bible school, the church camp, the weekend retreat, weekday religious classes, and youth and adult educational fellowships. In the major universities there were student religious foundations designed to give a religious basis to the social life of students as well as to give religious education.

The modern educational materials and methods were being adapted to religious education. Motion-picture projectors appeared in the churches. A well-equipped Sunday school had drawing and painting materials for young children, nursery school equipment, a room for dramatic presentations.

The larger churches had adult education programs, with study groups, training of laymen for leadership in the church, social action committees, and a variety of social fellowship groups.

A group of "foundation disciplines" were recognized as the basis for a curriculum of training for the profession of religious education. They were: theology, church history, philosophy, world history, psychology, and sociology. Sophisticated statements about religious education were being made by specialists in religious education who were scholars in the foundation disciplines. For example, the following is such a statement about the curriculum:

> The curriculum of Christian education may be organized by planning to involve learners, with all their varied needs and developing experience, in the church's ongoing study, fellowship, worship, work, witness, and mission — in which they are helped to come face-to-face with the gospel through study of the Bible and through the life of devotion; see the relevance of the gospel to the understanding of all of life — God, man, nature, and history; accept the promises and implications of the Christian faith, and become committed to membership in the worshipping and witnessing community and to full discipleship in the world.[5]

Thus the main body of Protestant churches in the United States have equipped themselves with an apparatus to maintain religious education and to develop it. They are continually and consciously working at the synthesis of affective with intellective processes to serve the educational functions of organized religion today.

The Traditionalist Countermovement. As the major Protestant denominations developed in these ways during this century, a variety of fundamentalist groups refused to go along with the modern religious education movement. They retained much of the teaching that had been standard for most Protestant churches during the nineteenth century. Their religious teaching was affective and didactic, and this found acceptance in the rural and working-class sectors of the population. They worked hard at developing youth programs, and attempted to bind their young people to the church by providing a full and attractive program of youth activities for Sundays, weekends, and weekdays that would satisfy the social as well as the religious needs. For instance, the program of the Assembly of God Church in a small war-boom town of Illinois was described as follows by the writer and a colleague. This church was founded in the war-boom community during World War II by a man-and-wife team who organized the workers to build their own building during free hours and to develop the most active church program in the community.

> This new church drew its members largely from among newcomers who had formerly been Baptists or Methodists — working-class people with a simple fundamentalist belief in the Scriptures. Since the Assembly of God was a tithing church, the money soon began to come in for a church building. In a few months, a lot was purchased on Main Street and excavation was begun, part of the labor being donated by church members. A one-story cinder-block building was constructed. The second story, containing the church auditorium proper, was to be constructed later. The building cost $6,000, and was free of debt shortly after it was completed.
>
> Attendance at the Sunday evening meeting, the principal meeting of the week, ran from a hundred to a hundred and forty. About seventy families, totaling some three hundred persons, became identified with the church, though none of them joined the church formally. The church was not "set in order" by the church authorities and hence could not receive members. This policy was purposeful, for with the future of the church uncertain it seemed better for the larger organization to carry the responsibility than for it to be turned over formally to the local people.
>
> At a typical Sunday evening service, there was a choir of twenty with an orchestra of four wind instruments. In the audience there were always several infants in arms and a dozen young children. The visitor coming in from the fresh outside air felt his nostrils contract with the sharp odor of human bodies.
>
> The preaching was preceded by an hour of testimonials interspersed with hymns. The piano played softly during the testimonials, to suggest what the next hymn would be. The testimonials began with people speaking rapidly and became faster and louder as they proceeded. At the end of the crescendo, the women would often weep.[6]

The songbook was entitled *Full Gospel Songs.* During a particular evening service the following songs were sung: "Are

You Washed in the Blood? " " Beulah Land," " I Love to Tell the Story," " Jesus Is Calling," " There Shall Be Showers of Blessing," " Whiter than Snow."

This church had activities scheduled five or six nights a week. For young people there was a Friday evening meeting, which competed with the Friday evening movie that had a special appeal for high school students. There was also a young people's orchestra, and the choir contained several teen-agers. Church services were for all the family. Young children were seldom left at home when parents went to church.

Although this kind of religious program has had a rapid growth among working-class people in the United States, it reaches only a relatively small proportion of that group. According to the *Yearbook of American Churches,* there are some three million members of Pentecostal-holiness-evangelical sects. Possibly half of the Southern Baptists might be placed in another traditionalist category. Even if those two groups are counted together, they would hardly make up more than 10 percent of working-class people. A majority of working-class people have no connection or at most only a nominal connection with a church, except where the Roman Catholic Church is strong.

Another type of sect attempts to maintain a social life that is largely separate from the larger society, and relies heavily on separate colleges and schools to do this. An example is the Seventh-day Adventist Church. An outside commentator sees this as an impossible task.

> The smaller and more evangelical Protestant sects, such as the Seventh-day Adventists and Mennonites, have continuously faced the dilemma: either to try to keep their young people from attending worldly and hence corrupting colleges, or to found their own and see them in the course of time become more worldly. One by one, however, the quainter severities distintegrate, and the general American youth culture, led by disc jockeys in addition to community-minded clergymen, takes over.[7]

However, a church leader sees the church schools and colleges as effective in keeping the group away from the evils of the world.

Though in many respects our institutions of learning have swung into worldly conformity, though step by step they have advanced toward the world, they are prisoners of hope. Fate has not so woven its meshes about their workings that they need to remain helpless and in uncertainty. If they will listen to His voice and follow in His ways, God will correct and enlighten them, and bring them back to their upright position of distinction from the world. . . .

I call upon our school faculties to use sound judgment and to work on a higher plane. Our educational facilities must be purified from all dross. Our institutions must be conducted on Christian principles if they would triumph over opposing obstacles. If they are conducted on worldly-policy plans, there will be a want of solidarity in the work, a want of farseeing spiritual discernment.[8]

The Parochial School. While most Protestant denominations were developing Sunday schools and then other elements of a separate religious education movement, the Roman Catholics developed the parochial school, and thus were in a position to weave religious education into general education. Some of the Lutheran groups, Calvinists, and fundamentalists have also built their own parochial schools, though these are not so widely available as are the Roman Catholic schools.

With the entire school program at its disposal, the church should be in an excellent position to make its own combination of the affective and intellective, and to adapt and adjust this combination in the light of experience. It has been estimated that approximately 45 percent of Catholic children attend parochial schools. Therefore it should be possible to study the effects of parochial school as distinguished from public school upon children reared as Catholics. Some studies of this sort have been made and the results are not fully conclusive. One Catholic writer comments as follows:

Studies indicate that in terms of internal commitment to basic Catholic values, graduates of Catholic schools do not show an appreciable difference from other Catholics. . . . Catholic school graduates are not, in comparison with the rest of the population, more or less mature, more or less prejudiced, more or less committed to the social teachings of the church, more or less involved in practicing reactionary or progressive community values.[9]

Father Andrew Greeley [10] has some evidence that the Catholic college may have more influence on the life orientation of students than does the elementary or secondary parochial school. In a study of college graduates, he found that Catholics who had attended Catholic colleges were more likely to say that religion offered them great life satisfaction than Catholics who had attended non-Catholic colleges. This was true whether the students had gone to a Catholic high school or not.

A careful study of the relation between religiosity and attendance in a non-Catholic religious school system has been made by Dr. Donald Ericson. He studied a group of students in grades 6, 7, 8, who attended fundamentalist day schools or churches, or both. He gave the boys and girls a test on their religious beliefs and their religious behavior. At the same time he obtained information on the extent of the church involvement of each child, parent religiosity, and home congeniality. He found that those who attended fundamentalist schools were no higher on a test of religiosity than those who did not. Those who scored highest in religiosity had high scores in parent religiosity combined with *either* high home congeniality or high church involvement, or both. He concludes: "There was no evidence that the sectarian school subjects were more religious than the public school subjects when home and church backgrounds were controlled. . . . The findings of the present study lend no support to the view that sectarian education is more conducive to religious development than is public education." [11]

On the other hand, a study [12] of persons reared in Seventh-day Adventist homes, from which some went to Seventh-day Adventist parochial schools while others did not, showed that there was a positive relationship between joining the church and the amount of parochial school education received. Since the membership requirements include rigid conduct rules, church membership is regarded as a moderately accurate index of individual commitment to the belief of the church.

Another exception to Ericson's finding is reported orally by Father Andrew Greeley from his current study of the effects of Catholic education. With parents of equal religiosity, it seems probable that children going to Catholic parochial schools are more religious than Catholic children attending non-Catholic schools.

Jewish Schools. Some of the Jewish churches have their own schools which operate weekday afternoons and evenings after the public school session, and are conducted by the local Jewish board of education or a similar group. The curriculum of such schools has been worked out with care and sophistication similar to that of the Protestant religious education movement. Pupils study Hebrew, Jewish history, the Jewish scriptures, as well as contemporary socioethical problems. These schools serve largely middle-class people, who are sensitive to the problem of synthesizing affective and intellective elements of education.

Released Time from Public Schools. In order to gain more time for religious education and to make it more effective, the religious education forces in a number of cities have banded together to provide classes in religion for public school children who are dismissed early one or more days a week and allowed to attend classes in religion if they so choose. Such a program has been declared unconstitutional by the United States Supreme Court if the public school uses its power to influence children to attend religious classes. However, "released time" programs are being conducted in a number of cities off of school property, by teachers employed by the churches.

Governing Influences in Religious Education

The great variety of provisions and programs of religious education in the United States should teach something about the conditions under which children will grow in the qualities that are goals of religious education. Still, it is difficult to draw sure conclusions. One source of the difficulty is the paucity of careful and systematic studies of the outcomes of religious education of one type as compared with another.

One conclusion is certain. The family is the principal source of the qualities that are sought through religious education. If one must choose between having families trained and anxious to do the work of religious education and having schools for this purpose, one should choose families. But it is no easy matter to motivate and to teach even the majority of families to do this task. It is also certain that the social class of a person determines to a considerable extent his life orientation, including some of the qualities aimed at in religious education. But social class works largely through the family. The social group past of a person has much to do with his life orientation. Thus in the Lenski study, Negro Protestants were quite different from white Protestants of the same social class. The experience of being one of a social group that has been stigmatized and exploited affects a person's life orientation. This also works largely but not entirely through the family.

But it is a form of cowardice for one who is interested in religious education to argue that, since so much depends upon the family, the ordinary and traditional apparatus of religious education should be abandoned. True, the family needs to be helped to do its part of the task, through educational and other influences directed at parents; but the church needs to work directly with the individual child, youth, and adult, and more effectively than in the past. This is especially important for the intellective aspect of religious education, for the family is not naturally good for intellective education.

The family works affectively through the close and intense emotional bonds that tie its members together. Any attempt at intellective analysis within the family is likely to be twisted by affective crosscurrents. However, the family can lay a good foundation for intellective education through the intellectual atmosphere it creates, especially for the preschool child, with the example of the father and the mother reading, answering the child's questions clearly and logically, and teaching the child an intellective style of language. The crisis in public education in the big cities of contemporary United States is caused partly by the intellectual deprivation that many children suffer due to poorly educated parents. Therefore, the family is important in making intellective education possible. But after the child is eight years old, the family needs to be supplemented by school and by church in the intellective education of its children.

The Tasks of Religious Education

An inquiry into the nature and outcome of education must ask what it aims to do, and how well it achieves these aims or objectives. The aims of religious education are broad and varied. Some churches stress certain of these aims to the exclusion of others. The language used to define and describe the aims may be one of religious terminology and symbolism, as the following:

> The mission of Christian education is to wait on the ceaseless ongoing action of the Triune God, as this action calls us forth, with penitent, thoughtful obedience, to participate in his reconciling work in all creation. The focus must be on what God is doing, not on what we are doing. It must be on what God is doing now. . . . The two great areas of experience where this reconciling work takes place and where the action of the Triune God can be most frequently encountered are in interpersonal relations and in the vast social complex of our society.[13]

The language to be used in this book is generally more akin to what is used in the behavioral sciences. We can speak of six broad objectives:

1. *Religiosity*. Religious beliefs and religious attitudes are sometimes taken as the *sine qua non* of religion. There is some evidence that the strength of religious belief is independent of the strength of opinion on other matters. Religious belief may be an isolated system, separate from other sets of attitudes and values. The ability to *worship* may be related to strength of religious belief. Most programs of religious education aim to help people recognize their need to worship, to discover satisfaction through worship, and to grow in the ability to worship. Worship is an end in itself, not an instrument for some other purpose.

2. *Church Loyalty*. Churches are concerned to win the loyalty of the new generation. The feeling of belonging to a church fellowship and of being loyal with and to others in the fellowship

contributes to religiosity, and also guarantees the continued life of the church.

3. *Otherworldliness.* The objective of teaching otherworldliness has different meanings for different churches. For some it is a belief in the imminent second coming of Christ. For others it is a faith in the existence of life after death. For still others it is a preference for religious, nonworldly values.

4. *Moral Character.* Most churches teach a code of ethical behavior as a part of religious behavior.

5. *Social Reform.* Achieving the Kingdom of God on earth is a task for those churches which believe in the brotherhood of man. They seek to change society and to change history through making religious people intelligently effective as they deal with the contemporary social and economic problems.

6. *World Outlook.* The ideal of world brotherhood is now regarded as the only possible alternative to world suicide. Churches with a missionary program work toward this goal, as do nonmissionary churches in a different way. The task of religious education in this connection is to teach knowledge and attitudes leading to the practice of world brotherhood.

Variant Stresses and Priorities. The various churches interpret these tasks variously. Religiosity and otherworldliness are emphasized by the fundamentalist sects as well as by substantial groups in the established denominations. Church loyalty is interpreted differently by different groups. Catholics work for loyalty to the Catholic Church, though not so much as formerly to the specific parish. The liberal Protestants do not set a high value on denominational loyalty, though they are concerned with loyalty to religious institutions. Fundamentalist Protestants are greatly concerned with loyalty to the local church. The various Jewish groups have different interpretations of loyalty to Jewish religion.

Moral character is universally stressed, but the various churches have rather different interpretations of what good character is, and of how it is developed.

The liberal Protestant, Catholic, and Jewish churches are pretty much in agreement on the significance of social reform and world brotherhood, and are working at these goals through education of their adult and younger members.

The three objectives or tasks listed last in the six above — moral character, social reform, and world outlook — have been worked at more systematically from the explicit educational point of view than have the first three. Also, they have been treated as objectives requiring a combination of intellective and affective education. Though not necessarily the more important in the eyes of religionists, these three have been more amenable to work by institutional and ecumenical groups. Each of them, then, will be the subject of a special chapter in this book.

Evaluation of Religious Education

Everyone who is doing something he considers important must stop occasionally to take stock of what he has done and what he has accomplished. This is the elementary form of evaluation. It is done informally or formally by every church, business, school, government, and it is done usually less fully by every family and every individual.

Wherever the product or the objective is something visible or tangible, evaluation generally consists of looking at the product and judging how good it is.

In the field of education there has been a good deal of effort at evaluation. There has been much experimentation and trial of new ideas and new methods in education. Someone has to judge whether the new is better than the old. This kind of judgment is best made with the aid of visible, objective evidence. The procedure of evaluation is to provide the visible, objective evidence upon which such judgments can be made.

In a conference on Evaluation and Christian Education, Elizabeth Hagen gave the following general description of evaluation:

> An educational program is usually undertaken to achieve one or more of the following three purposes:
>
> To produce changes in the behavior of people that otherwise would not occur.
>
> To produce changes in the behavior of people more quickly.

To produce a greater degree of change in the behavior of people.

The word "behavior" in this context is used very broadly. It includes knowledge, understanding, ways of thinking, skills, attitudes, values, interests and feelings as well as the verbal, non-verbal, and physical actions of a person. The behavioral changes that we want to effect through our educational program provide the framework for building the curriculum for the program and selecting the learning experiences and teaching methods for the program. The curriculum, learning activities, and methods of teaching are means to an end — not an end in and of themselves.

The changes in behavior that we want to produce are sometimes called objectives, sometimes aims, sometimes goals of our educational program. In educational circles the words "objectives," "goals," and "aims" are used interchangeably. In order to make my meaning clear, I would like to describe my use of these terms. If we can consider Christian education as a whole first, we find that it has a philosophy which serves to shape and give general direction to it. Within this philosophical framework, we usually find a statement expressed in very general and global terms of the overall purpose of the program. For example, in the booklet, *The Objective of Christian Education for Senior High Young People,* one finds the following statement: "The objective of Christian education is to help persons to be aware of God's self-disclosure and seeking love in Jesus Christ and to respond in faith and love — to the end that they may know who they are and what their human situation means, grow as sons of God rooted in the Christian community, live in the Spirit of God in every relationship, fulfill their common discipleship in the world, and abide in the Christian hope."

Essentially this statement reflects the ultimate goal of Christian education. I tend to use the word "goal" to refer to this kind of general, overall purpose of an education program. Persons in an education program do not reach this ultimate goal all of a sudden. They progress toward the goal through a series of stages. The identification of the stages of progress I call the general objectives of the program and the behaviors that go to make up each stage of progress, I call the specific objectives.

To summarize my usage of terms, let us use the term "ultimate goal" to denote the overall purpose of Christian education of all kinds. Let us use the term "general objective" for the purposes of the parts that make up the total program; i.e., for senior high young people or for junior high young people. Since each of these is a part of the total program, the general objectives for each part are more specific definitions of the general goal that give better guidelines both to the persons administering the program and to the learner in the program. Within each of the major parts of the total program, different kinds of experiences are provided which have been selected because it is believed that these experiences will help to produce specific changes in the behavior of the learner. These specific changes in the behavior of the learner, I call specific objectives.

Evaluation Defined. Let us assume at this point, that we at least have an understanding of the ultimate goal and general objectives of our educational program. As we carry through our educational activities, sooner or later we find ourselves wondering whether we are achieving our goal. In other words, we want to determine the effectiveness of the educational program; we want to evaluate our educational program.

The word "evaluation" is used here to mean the systematic gathering of evidence concerning certain selected attributes of the educational program and arriving at a value judgment on the basis of the evidence collected about the worthwhileness of the educational program. Evaluation then is a process that involves measurement and valuing. . . .

The process of evaluation involves three distinct aspects:

1. Selecting and defining the attributes to be evaluated (the "what" of evaluation).
2. Developing and applying procedures that will describe these attributes truly and accurately (the "how" of evaluation).
3. Synthesizing the evidence into a final judgment of worth (the interpretation and use of results).[14]

For example, in evaluating a particular course or unit in a program of religious education, one would:

1. Decide what is to be evaluated. State the objectives of the course or activity to be evaluated.

2. Devise appropriate methods for getting evidence about the achievement of the objectives that have been stated. Such instruments as tests, questionnaires, interviews, and records of observations may be used.

3. Analyze the evidence.

4. Draw conclusions about the value of the course or activity that is being studied.

Evaluating Religious Personality Growth. One of the major objectives of Christian education is to foster growth in Christian personality. Personality is visible, personality growth is visible, and Christian personality growth is visible.

If we can describe Christian personality growth in observable terms, we have the criteria that we need in order to test our methods of work. Good methods of Christian education will lead to greater personality growth in Christian terms, or to more desirable forms of personality.

Personality consists of four broad categories of behavior: (1) knowledge and understanding; (2) habits; (3) value attitudes; (4) personal qualities.

Growth in Christian personality consists in growth of these four categories and a special kind of growth that is defined by the Christian saints, prophets, and leaders, past and present.

In order to evaluate a program of education that has this for its goal, it is natural to collect evidence on the changes in these four categories of behavior which take place in boys and girls and men and women who are members of the church fellowship. We must collect evidence concerning the changes that take place in a person in his knowledge of the Bible, habits of Christian charity, attitudes toward other people, and his moral conscience. If this were a simple matter, no doubt it would have been done long ago. But the *Christian* aspects of personality tend to be intangible, difficult to measure, and so complex that the scientist prefers to turn to easier problems, such as the measurement of a person's vocabulary, or of his reading ability, or of his arithmetic knowledge.

Nevertheless, we can make an important and useful start by simply listing some of the *Christian* elements in the four categories of personality behavior named above. And we can suggest ways of getting objective and, preferably, quantitative evidence concerning the degree to which a person possesses these characteristics.

The problem of measurement of the intangibles of religion is dramatized by the following incident of doubtful authenticity. William was a thirteen-year-old boy who lived with his widowed mother in a small Midwestern city a decade ago. He was not much of a scholar, and he did not care for school. He had a shock of red hair, and, due to a childhood accident, he had only one eye. His friends called him Bill.

Bill's teacher told the class one afternoon: "I want you all to invite your parents to come to school tomorrow morning to hear me give you a test to measure your spiritual IQ. I learned this test at summer school last summer and I want your parents to know about it. And I'm going to give a prize of a five-dollar bill to the boy or girl who does best in this test. Class dismissed."

Bill neglected to tell his mother of this invitation, and he was not at all anxious to take the test. In fact, he overslept the next morning, and complained of a stomachache when his mother woke him up. But she said: "Now, Willy, none of that. You get right up and get to school." Bill dawdled through breakfast, but his mother pushed him along, and, then, just as he was leaving for school, she remembered that she needed bread for lunch. She gave him a dime to bring home a loaf of bread at noon.

Bill started out for school. When he came to the railroad tracks he looked one way and another, hoping that a long freight train would delay him. But there was no train in sight. He crossed the tracks and then he had an idea. He would buy the bread now, instead of later when he was on his way home. This took him a block out of his way to go to the store. When he arrived at school the yard was bare. Not a child was in sight. He was really late.

Entering the school building, Bill tiptoed up the stairway and looked through the open door of his classroom. There were mothers and fathers sitting on chairs all around the edges of the room. Well, there was no way of getting out of it, and Bill lowered his head and walked quietly to his empty seat.

"William," said his teacher, "you are just in time. All the other boys and girls have taken the test, and now it is your turn. Pay attention." She held up one finger. Bill held up two fingers.

She held up her hand with three fingers showing. Bill held up his fist. She picked up an apple which was on her desk. Bill held up his loaf of bread.

The teacher exclaimed: "William, that was very good. I'm surprised and delighted at your spiritual insight. You have done better than anybody else. You have won the five-dollar prize. I wish your mother could see you now." Then she turned to the class. "Now, boys and girls, go out for recess. I know your parents would like to have me explain the meaning of this test to them."

After the pupils had streamed out of the room, she spoke to the puzzled parents. "This was a test of knowledge and insight into religious symbolism," she said. "That boy, William, showed a surprising understanding, much more than I have thought was possible in his case. It goes to show how important an objective test is. No doubt some of you understand these symbols, but perhaps others do not. I'll tell you what the test means.

"I started with one finger, which signified the Deity. William held up two fingers, to show that there are two in the Godhead, Father and Son. I showed three fingers to signify the third element, the Holy Ghost. William held up his closed hand to show that they were three in one. I held up the apple as the symbol of man's fall from grace, and William held up the loaf of bread which is the bread of life, the saving grace of God. So you see what remarkable spiritual understanding that boy has."

When Bill reached home that noon his mother asked, "How was school this morning, Willy?" "Pretty good. Better than I expected," Bill said. "Look what I won." And he showed the five-dollar bill. "My goodness, boy! Tell me how you got that," said his mother, in some alarm.

"Well, it was this way," Bill said. "When I got there the teacher said I had to take this test. She held up one finger to show that I had only one eye. I held up two fingers to show that my one eye was as good as her two. She held up three fingers to show that we had only three eyes between us. I shook my fist to show what I would do to her if she didn't quit that kind of business. She picked up an apple to throw at me. I held up my loaf of bread to protect myself. And she gave me the five-dollar bill to lay off."

It is indeed desirable that we know for certain what is evidence that a pupil is accomplishing the objectives of religious education.

A Practical Approach to Evaluation

This introduction to the process of evaluating religious education is enough to indicate some of the complexity involved. Tests of knowledge and skills — the easiest tests to make — are not of great value in religious education. Measurement of attitudes and values is more important, but is also more difficult. Not much progress has yet been made in evaluating the outcomes of religious education. Some of the most important outcomes are usually stated in quasi-theological terms, and are difficult or impossible to translate into terms of observable human behavior.

Probably religious education programs will have to be evaluated largely by a procedure that has great strength for use in complex situations, but is sometimes misused. This procedure is that of judgment by competent and objective judges. An example of this procedure in evaluating a program of Sunday school lessons for youth of given high school age is as follows:

A team of experienced and competent people is called in to evaluate the program. They are provided with a written statement of the objectives of the program, made by the director and his associates in the program. They discuss this statement with the director and staff of the Sunday school. They ask for evidence that the objectives are being accomplished. They examine whatever evidence is given them. They observe the Sunday school and talk with pupils and teachers. Eventually the team discusses its observations and makes its judgment.

In this procedure everything depends on the quality of the judges. If they are narrow, provincial, limited in experience, or prejudiced, their evaluation will be incompetent. Yet if they are broad, tolerant, experienced, and wise, their judgment will be better than anything that could be obtained by tests.

II. THE CHURCH AND THE HUMAN LIFE CYCLE

The notion of man's existence as a journey or pilgrimage through time appears in many different centuries and places in the panorama of human history. The world's great religions have used it. We see it in one form in Bunyan's *The Pilgrim's Progress*. In another form we have the Oriental concept of transmigration of the soul through various animal forms until the end of existence is attained.

For the psychologist — the scientist of the soul — the journey through life is an attractive concept, and we find the human life cycle treated as a psychological problem by such modern integrative thinkers as Erich Fromm, Charlotte Buehler, and Erik Erikson.

The essential idea is that life is a sequence in which the experience and the achievement or failure at one stage lays the basis for achievement or failure at later stages, so that whatever a person does or experiences at one place in his life cycle has consequences for later stages.

Since education is a process in which there is always something going before and something following after, it is natural to think of education in terms of progress through a life cycle. Secular education is a set of experiences that carry a person through his secular life. Religious education can be thought of as a set of experiences that carry a person through his religious life.

Successful education means helping a person to go through life with more competence than he would otherwise have. Religious education is a matter of helping a person to go through life with more religious competence than he would otherwise have.

Lifelong Education. In the contemporary world it is no longer useful to think of life as consisting of a succession of three stages: play (for infants and children), study (for children and adolescents), and work (for adults). This was an appropriate classification when children led a life of play during infancy which tapered off while study replaced it during middle childhood, with study in turn giving way to work in adolescence or early adulthood. Nowadays, most adults have to go on studying in order to keep up with their changing jobs, and they ought to go on studying in order to be effective citizens and parents. It is more useful, now, to think of life as a rope woven of different materials differing in thickness during the various stages. In childhood the heaviest strand is play, but there is some study and there may be some work. In adolescence the strand of study thickens while the strand of play becomes thinner, and the strand of work may grow thicker. In adulthood, the strand of work thickens at the expense of the play and study strands, but they remain important and essential parts of life. As a person grows older, his work may thin out, and the play strand may thicken, with the strand of study remaining, but devoted to purposes other than a person's vocational improvement.

The Church and Adult Education. The church is one of the principal educative agencies for all ages. For adults it may become *the* principal agency. In a recent survey of people who were taking part in adult education as learners,[15] it was found that churches and synagogues sponsored 21 percent of the courses that were taken — exactly the same proportion being sponsored by colleges and universities. Many of the courses sponsored by churches lay outside the field of religion, specifically defined as such. Fifteen percent of the courses taken dealt with religion, 37 percent with vocation, 16 percent with hobbies and recreation, and 11 percent with academic subjects. Thus religion was in third place as a subject area. It was estimated that 3,260,000 adults took courses sponsored by churches and synagogues in the year commencing June, 1961. A total of 23 million adults, or 20 per-cent of the adult population, took courses that were defined as adult education. None of these persons was a full-time student.

The Developmental Task Concept

In this chapter we shall think of passage through the life cycle as the achievement of a series of developmental tasks, and we shall ask whether there is a series of religious developmental tasks that a person must achieve if he is to live a competent religious life.

The concept of a developmental task comes from study of biological and social organisms. Whether we study man as a biological organism or man as a member of a social organism, we are struck with the fact that there are some essential steps in growth that have an inevitable order and a fixed time of appearance in the course of human physical or social development.

For example, in the development of the human embryo there is a fixed sequence in which the major features of the embryo appear. The eyes, ears, mouth, and nose arise in certain places and in a certain order on what was at first only the head end of the developing fetus. It might be said that the human body has a series of developmental tasks to achieve as it develops in the womb from an early stage as a mass of dividing germ cells to the full-formed baby ready to be born. Furthermore, a distortion of the developmental process has evil consequences for later development if it occurs at a critical time or place. For example, experiments with animal embryos, such as rabbits, have shown that if the embryo rabbit, developing in its mother's body, is probed at the spot on the head *where* the eyes are about to develop and *when* the eyes are about to develop, the eyes do not develop properly, and the sequence of later development of other organs is disturbed. Yet if the same spot on the embryo's head is probed a few days earlier, before that area becomes activated for development, the spot heals and the eyes develop with little or no difficulty and the later developmental process is not disturbed.

Thus there is a critical time and place in biological development when the event must take place if development is to proceed normally from then on.

In the development of the individual in society there is also a sequence of societal developmental tasks. These are seen most clearly in a simple society where the generations arise and pass without disturbance from social forces that induce change, so that the society expects the new generation to repeat the patterns laid down in the past. For example, in the traditional Hopi Indian society, the Hopi mother unstrapped her baby from the cradle board at a certain age when it was proper for him to learn to stand and walk. Thus he had the developmental task of learning to walk at a certain age. Other tasks of growing up followed in order, until the child was ready for his first initiation at the age of six or eight. Here the time period had a latitude of a couple of years, so that a group of children could be put through the ceremony together. They were brought into the sacred cave, or kiva, in a religious ceremony, in which they were taught that the kachinas — the supernatural beings that they had feared and revered because they whipped bad children and brought presents for good children — were really their own uncles dressed in masks, and from now on they, as initiates, would know this but must not tell the uninitiated younger children.

After this developmental task the next major one for boys was the second initiation, at about thirteen or fourteen, into a religious society. The boy had been selected sometime before and had been taught by his sponsor the sacred lore of the society. He learned that each society had its own particular job to do in keeping the Hopi people in good and fruitful relations with the supernatural world. He was required to learn his part in his religious society, so that the life of the tribe could go on. If he should fail to memorize the chant or to learn his particular steps in the sacred dance, the sun would not turn back north at the time of the winter solstice, or the corn seeds would not sprout after being planted, or the August rains would not come to ripen the corn and the beans, or some other natural catastrophe would occur, all because he and his brothers in his religious society had not kept their part of the bargain with the spirits that governed the universe.

The next task for boys and girls was that of choosing a mate and getting married at about the age of sixteen. Thereafter the girl had to learn to have her first baby and how to give it a good start in life. The tasks of the adult part of the Hopi life cycles were not so sharply defined or so dramatically reinforced as these early ones, perhaps because the simple life of the society did not require other major learnings.

The good Hopi, then, was one who had learned his developmental tasks as a child and youth in the right sequence and manner and so was able to contribute his share to the preservation of the society.

From these examples, we can define a developmental task as a kind of behavior that must be learned at a certain time period in the human life cycle; success leads to success in later tasks; failure leads to failure in later tasks.

Driving Forces Behind Developmental Tasks. The force that impels a person to achieve a developmental task may be one of three kinds. At first, the forces are all biological, and the tasks are those of biological development during the embryonic period and the first few months of life when the human is still primarily an animal. Biological forces continue to be basic in tasks concerned primarily with biological behavior, such as the development of boy-girl relations in adolescence, the adjustment of women to menopause, and the adjustment of men and women to declining physical and sensory capacities after about the age of sixty.

Another motivating force is that of social expectation. When society expects a young man to choose a vocation and earn a living, he feels this keenly and generally obeys the social expectation. When society expects a young adult to cast his first vote, he takes his citizenship more seriously than before, especially in societies that make a ceremony of First Voters Day.

The third motivating force is the self-concept, or the individual aspiration. A person can and does set developmental tasks for himself, though perhaps it is more accurate to say that he experiences the driving forces of his biological maturation and the pressures of his social environment as cues for the performance of developmental tasks, and relies upon his own self-concept, ego-ideal, or aspiration to determine the form and level of his achievement of the particular task. For example, one person will finish elementary school and feel satisfied with this performance of the developmental task of completing his formal education, whereas another person with a different self-concept will not be content until he achieves a Ph.D. degree.

In a complex and modern society the self-concept or personal aspiration is extremely important in the achievement of almost every developmental task, since the society permits many forms and levels of achievement of most tasks. This fact complicates the problem of the educational system. In a simple, unchanging society such as that of the traditional Hopi, the educational system had only to provide for teaching a few basic tasks that would be learned more or less equally well by everybody. There was not much variety in the self-concept of the Hopi children of a given generation. But the contemporary society has an enormous variety of social expectations, some conflicting with others, and the individual self-concept is so malleable that the educational system must concern itself with the forming and development of the self-concept, as well as with the training of the person in accordance with his self-concept.

Ethical Neutrality of the Developmental Task Principle. Some thoughtful people have pointed out that the developmental task principle has no provision for the concept of the human being as by nature sinful. This is true. The human being is seen as initially an amoral organism that is made into a moral person by his family and other persons. His biological drives or impulses are not necessarily sinful or evil. They can lead him to sin or bad behavior. But they can also lead him to good behavior. Therefore, wholesome development is seen not so much as learning to control and inhibit impulses because they lead to evil behavior, but rather as learning to direct impulses toward good behavior. Thus a person who is "impulsive" can be a good or a bad person, depending on whether his impulses are good or bad. A person who is basically friendly and trustful of others does not have to flagellate himself so as to conquer his "sinful nature." On the other hand, a person who is basically hostile and mistrustful of others must "wrestle with himself" to keep from acting as a bad person.

We suppose that the difference between these two persons is due to the way they were reared or taught or influenced by the people around them as they proceeded through life.

The developmental tasks are ethically neutral. They are "given" by the body and by society. But a person's performance of his developmental tasks is judged morally by his society and by himself in accord with ethical principles. He is a "good" person as a member of a peer group of adolescents because he behaves in ways defined as "good" by the society. She is a "good" mother of her children because she treats her children in socially approved ways. A good society takes advantage of human impulses and human growth to produce people who are good. A bad society uses the same forces of behavior and growth to produce bad people.

Developmental Tasks of a Theocratic Society. In a theocratic society there are a series of well-defined religious developmental tasks, and a system of religious education is organized or grows up around these tasks. For example, it would be fairly easy to describe the education of a Hebrew child in the generations preceding King David in terms of a set of religious developmental tasks combined with a set of economic developmental tasks, the two sets being somewhat intertwined. To come closer to our time and situation, there are some rural Christian sects that are essentially theocratic and that seek to seal themselves off from the outside world through their system of rearing and educating children. Examples are the Mennonite and Amish communities. They keep the religious and the secular education of their children as far as possible in their own communal hands. This education centers about religious and economic developmental tasks. The children learn to attend church in appropriate dress; they take the steps of religious instruction. They marry according to the precepts of the church. The cycle of religious life is closely ordered both to the cycle of economic life and to the life cycle.

Even in the churches that participate more fully in the contemporary urban civilization there are some specifically religious developmental tasks. Baptism is such a task, whether it be for infants or for adolescents when they become members of the church. The churches that have confirmation or membership classes of younger adolescents are setting a religious developmental task for them. The Bar Mitzvah for Jewish boys continues to be a significant developmental task. Some pastors, priests, and rabbis make marriage a religious developmental task by requiring the couple to accept pastoral counseling.

Still, there are not enough of these specifically religious developmental tasks, and they are not freighted with enough social and personal significance, to allow them to become the main body of religious education in a modern society.

Religious Dimension of Developmental Tasks. Both secular and religious education can profit from moving with the forces of biological, social, and psychological development in the timing and choosing of educative experiences. Whenever a person meets a challenge in life that he *must* work at, there is a possibility for education. If the successful working at this challenge depends at least partly upon religious behavior, there is a possibility for religious education.

For example, if it is a fact of our society that boys and girls at age sixteen to eighteen are especially interested in questions of the "philosophy of life" type, then it is true that thinking about and formulating a "philosophy of life" is a developmental task at that age. And since religion is concerned with a person's "philosophy of life" (his scale of values, world view, concept of the nature of man and the nature of history), religious instruction dealing with philosophy of life should be timed to coincide with the tendency to work on this developmental task that exists in our society. Such instruction is likely to be more effective at age sixteen to eighteen than at age fourteen or twenty-two. The youth is not yet " ready " at age fourteen to grasp the significance of the task; at twenty-two he has already come to some kind of achievement of the task, for better or for worse, and is now more concerned with other tasks, such as getting married and starting a family, or preparing himself for a complex occupational role.

Our proposal, then, is to examine the developmental tasks that arise in our society through the operations of biological development, societal pressures, and personal aspirations; to select the ones that have the most important religious dimensions; and to organize religious education so as to supply the religious dimension at the time and place when it can be most effectively taught.

The Selection of Developmental Tasks for Religious Treatment. There are two ways by which developmental tasks can be selected and defined for religious treatment. One is to take the statement of developmental tasks used in secular education and to select those which have the greatest religious dimensions. For instance, one might take the list of tasks set forth in Havighurst's *Human Development and Education.*[16]

The life cycle is divided by Havighurst into a series of stages, and the tasks of each stage are defined as shown in the following example for the period of middle childhood, from age six to twelve.

The developmental tasks of middle childhood are:

1. Learning physical skills necessary for ordinary games.
2. Building wholesome attitudes toward oneself as a growing organism.
3. Learning to get along with age-mates.
4. Learning an appropriate masculine or feminine social role.
5. Developing fundamental skills in reading, writing, and calculating.
6. Developing concepts necessary for everyday living.
7. Developing conscience, morality, and a scale of values.
8. Achieving personal independence.
9. Developing attitudes toward social groups and institutions.

When children's performances in these tasks are rated on a scale of achievement, it is found that there is a strong tendency for good performance in one task to go along with good performance in other tasks. That is, a child who does well in one task is likely to do well in other tasks also. This suggests that the church or the school or any other agency that is concerned with helping children achieve their developmental tasks may usefully work along a broad front of developmental tasks. A church that is concerned with helping children develop conscience, morality, and a scale of values may find it advisable also to help children with their task of learning to get along with age-mates or of achieving personal independence. Although one could carry this inference too far, such as expecting the church to teach the three R's in Sunday school, it certainly seems desirable to work through the church for the achievement of most of the developmental tasks, for most of them have an ethical quality, and the church is concerned that they be achieved in accordance with religious standards.

The goal of performance for a certain developmental task, such as that of developing attitudes toward social groups and institutions, is set by the social group in which a person lives, and also by his own aspirations. The church is concerned with the ethical goals of the community, and with the aspirations of the individual. Consequently, there are *religious performance goals* for many of the developmental tasks that are somewhat different in quality from the performance goals set by the community, which is not perfect by the standards of religious ethics.

To illustrate the religious performance goals, let us look at the developmental tasks of another age level—that of middle age, about thirty to fifty.

The developmental tasks of middle age are:

1. Reaching the peak in one's work career.
2. Setting adolescent children free and helping them to become happy and responsible adults.
3. Discovering new satisfactions in relations with one's spouse.
4. Creating a comfortable home.
5. Achieving mature civic and social responsibility.

6. Becoming or maintaining oneself as an active member of a church, a club, or an organization.
7. Accepting and adjusting to the physiological changes of middle age.

A church with an active educational program for adults might provide activities and social groups that would help the individual with all these tasks. Probably tasks Nos. 5 and 6, dealing with social responsibility and with church and other forms of organizational activity, would be of most explicit concern to the church, through its adult study groups and its laymen's organizations for social civic action and through its own organizational structure with vestrymen, members of the church council, members of the women's society, ushers, church school teachers, etc. There might also be study groups dealing with adolescence, with home planning and decoration, and with the health problems of adults. While these do not have an explicitly religious or ethical dimension, they are likely to appear in a broad church program of adult education. In addition, the pastoral counseling function of the church will very probably involve the pastor in helping some of his members with one or more of their middle-age tasks.

The Case of Mr. Rogers. The way in which pastoral counseling and the church program may be related to adult developmental tasks is illustrated by the hypothetical case of a man of forty-seven, Mr. Rogers. The pastor found him in the local hospital, waiting for diagnosis and treatment of a painful but obscure condition of his back. Mr. Rogers had been pretty much a nominal member of the church. He was a salesman in a department store, had three children aged twenty, seventeen, and fourteen, and his wife was active in the women's society of the church. Mr. Rogers stayed in the hospital for ten days while the doctors tried vainly to find something organically wrong with him. This gave time for three long talks, which Mr. Rogers continued by making appointments with the pastor at the church office.

A good deal of the talk centered around Mr. Rogers' dissatisfaction with his work. He was thinking of going to the local university to take graduate work in economics, with the aim of teaching in college. While discussing this matter, the pastor found out the following apparently unrelated information. There was a good deal of conflict in the home between parents and children. The latter were declaring their independence in ways that disturbed Mrs. Rogers, who tried to " mother " them more than they wanted. Mr. Rogers also was not altogether pleased with the educational and other choices his children were making, but he was more inclined than Mrs. Rogers to allow them to take responsibility for themselves. This brought him into arguments with his wife at times. She was becoming moody, sometimes irritable and sometimes depressed. This may have been due to the beginning of menopause. Anyway, Mr. Rogers found himself looking for excuses to go out alone at night or to stay downtown after work.

Mr. Rogers was worried about the costs of college education for his children. He could not afford to quit his job for further study. As a citizen he kept up on current social and civic issues by reading a liberal magazine as well as the local newspaper and the more popular magazines. He thought of himself as a critical analyst of the present state of affairs. As a teacher, he thought he might have more time to study and more influence. Meanwhile, he had declined to serve on the board of directors of a settlement house in the city. In his leisure time Mr. Rogers preferred to read. He had lost interest in his house and garden, which he had formerly kept in excellent condition with the help of his children. He formerly enjoyed tennis, but this affected his back, he believed, and he had cut it out.

The pastor concluded that the decision to change jobs was symptomatic of a general lack of success with the developmental tasks of middle age, and that Mr. Rogers would not find what he wanted in this way, even if he could afford to quit his present job. Mr. Rogers accepted a position on the social action committee of the church and became an active and leading member. He and his wife joined a discussion group on " Adolescents Grow Up " which the church sponsored. Mr. and Mrs. Rogers spent more time together, at church and elsewhere. After a year Mr.

Rogers realized one day that his back had not pained him for a long time. He began to take an interest again in his garden and started some new rose plantings.

The pastor, thinking over his year's work with Mr. Rogers, concluded that the change for the better was due to improvement in the performance of several developmental tasks, which mutually interacted to raise Mr. Rogers' morale. The church had been a useful, if not essential, agent in these changes.

Psychosocial Tasks with a Religious Dimension. Another procedure of possible interest to religious education is that of choosing one *dominant* or *crucial* developmental task at a given level, and concentrating on the religious dimension of its achievement. For this procedure we can get a lead from the analysis of the life cycle made by Erik Erikson into a series of eight psychosocial tasks.[17] Proceeding on the basis of psychoanalytic theory, Erikson defines the tasks and their timing as follows:

Sense of trust	Early childhood
Autonomy	Early childhood
Initiative and inner control	Early and middle childhood
Industry	Middle childhood
Identity	Adolescence
Intimacy	Early adulthood
Responsibility for social welfare (generativity)	Middle age
Integrity	Later maturity

In Erikson's book *Young Man Luther,*[18] we see a brilliant exposition of the problems a great man and a religious hero had in achieving his psychosocial tasks of identity, intimacy, and generativity. His biography as a religious leader was structured by his peculiar combination of religious experience and delayed achievement in these three tasks. But one would hardly build a program of religious education on the unique experience of Luther. Better to build it on the normal experience of average people going through the life cycle.

To do this, we have made the following analysis of the life

cycle into a series of Dominant Psychosocial Tasks, each of which has a major religious dimension.

Dominant Psychosocial Tasks and the Church Program

The following treatment of psychosocial developmental tasks is only one of a number of ways of thinking about stages of human development. Although there are ten tasks in this list, there is no " correct " number. Nor are there scientifically established age limits for the various tasks.

Tasks	*Age*
1. Formation of a moral conscience	four to eight
2. Becoming a sociable person	six to twelve
3. Learning moral autonomy based on moral principles	eight to sixteen
4. Achieving identity	sixteen to twenty-four
5. Achieving intimacy	twenty to thirty
6. Exercising responsible parenthood	twenty to forty-five
7. Becoming a productive worker	twenty to forty
8. Exercising responsible citizenship	thirty to sixty
9. Using practical wisdom for the social welfare	fifty to seventy
10. Disengaging from active life with personal and social responsibility	sixty and up

1. *Formation of a Moral Conscience.* By the age of four the child has begun to internalize moral rules. He has been taught the meaning of good and bad behavior by the approval and disapproval, the rewards and punishments, that his parents and teachers have given to him. Now it is time for him to control his anger, to leave other people's property alone, to respect his mother's order to leave the cookie jar unopened, to tell the truth. He learns moral self-control partly through his unconscious imitation of his parents and older brothers and sisters, and partly through being taught the consequences of good and bad behavior.

The church has limited direct contact with the child at this age. It affects the child's conscience mainly by instructing parents in the ways to rear their children. However, by the time a child is going to church school, there is some opportunity for teaching him the bases for distinguishing right from wrong. Church school lessons can point out how a child's behavior harms or benefits other people, how what he does and says has consequences for the welfare of others.

2. *Becoming a Sociable Person.* The child moves out from the family circle into the world of his age-mates as he enters school and spends increasing amounts of time with people who are not of his immediate family. This is a move from a situation in which the child gets emotional security from his close relations with his mother and other family members into a new world where he must make a place for himself among a group of age-mates or peers. The child must learn the give-and-take of social life. He learns how to treat friends. He learns what it means to play fair in games. He learns ways of approaching strangers, shy or bold, standoffish or friendly.

In more nearly religious terms, the child begins to learn the meaning of *agapē,* or Christian love. He learns to forgive other people and to ask forgiveness. He learns how to handle disagreements by techniques other than quarreling. He appreciates how he can contribute to the welfare of others, and how they contribute to his own well-being. In brief, he forms his social personality.

The church school and the other church organizations for children can play an important part in helping the child at the age of middle childhood to become a *charitable* person. The church can influence the child not only by direct teaching but also in the opportunities the church makes for social give-and-take in an atmosphere provided by its ethical principles.

3. *Learning Moral Autonomy Based on Moral Principles.* Although moral responsibility starts with the development of an internal moral conscience, this is at first simply the incorporated warning and rewarding voice of the parents. The child is not a morally autonomous person; instead, he is an immature replica of the parents, voicing their values and prejudices. From about

the age of eight until his middle teens, at any rate, the child gradually learns what moral principles are and what their justification is, and he is generally in a position to organize his own moral behavior around these principles. He becomes able to apply his moral principles as a guide to his behavior in new situations for which he has no ready-made answers.

The child learns to conform to moral principles, but this does not make him a *conformist.* His conformity to *principles* prevents him from conforming to the social pressures of the moment. He has the ability to weigh alternatives and to make choices in the light of what he can foresee as the probable consequences of his behavior.

The church can exercise a major influence on this element of moral character by its teaching in church school and youth organizations. Some churches consciously encourage youth to *intellectualize* moral conduct, while other churches play this element down and teach a more specific behavioral code in which right behavior is previously defined and taught as a commandment. In either case, the later elementary school and early high school years are the ones that count in the structuring of moral character.

4. *Achieving Identity.* During adolescence the youth becomes a person in his own right. He does this in four ways: he learns to accept his body and his sex role; he decides upon his occupation; he becomes emotionally independent of his parents and other adults; and he develops a philosophy of life. The result of successful accomplishment is that he moves into adulthood with a sure feeling of who he is and where he wants to go in life. The church can help in all four of these aspects of achieving identity. Through its youth groups and its youth leaders the church can help a boy or girl learn what it means to be a young man or a young woman, and to decide upon a vocation that will have religious as well as secular values.

A necessary condition for achieving identity is confidence in oneself and fidelity or faith in and commitment to the values of one's society. The adolescent in contemporary American society is likely to approach this task with a good deal of self-doubt and doubt about the worthiness of his own society. The reasons for this condition are two. First, the boy (or girl) of twelve to fifteen finds himself coping with a highly complex situation. He is under pressure to do well in school and to make school choices that will lead him to or away from college, at an age when he is hardly ready to choose an occupation. He is expected to earn his own self-esteem through his school achievement and through his social sophistication with the opposite sex. He can no longer rely on his family to give him assurance that he is a worthy person. He is very much on his own in the adolescent society and in the competitive high school scholarship race. As a sensitive and fairly intelligent youngster, hardly more than a child, he is keenly aware of his unreadiness to face the complex world.

Second, the young adolescent has doubts about the basic goodness of the society around him. He sees nations threatening wars of nuclear destruction. At the same time he reads about the evil side of human nature in the realistic literature that is so popular in school courses and even in some church youth groups. He reads such books as *The Catcher in the Rye* and *Lord of the Flies,* and other examples of the so-called " sick " literature. He is bathed in the contemporary mood of frankness and social self-criticism. These experiences, which are very difficult to avoid in the middle-class urban segment of society, tend to raise grave doubts and a certain amount of cynicism about modern society rather than the fidelity to society and its ideals that is necessary for the achievement of a positive identity in this society.

A rather natural reaction to this state of affairs is a retreat to a kind of privatistic life, in which he does not commit himself to anything in the adult society, but leads a life with a few choice friends that emphasizes private, nonsocial and nonaffirmative actions, such as enjoying modern art and modern music, and discussing philosophical problems in an unreal context. In short, the youth moves toward the beatnik syndrome.

The church has an opportunity to intervene at this age, with a teaching and a social situation that leads to greater faith in self and society. It can do this by wise choice of church school teachers and youth leaders who are themselves positive, affirmative people and whose example of warm personal relations with boys and girls helps the young people to gain confidence in themselves.

As the young people move on from the age period of twelve to fifteen to that of the later teens, the church can assist them to formulate their philosophy of life. They can meet in church school and youth groups to discuss personal and social problems and to work out their own codes of social ethics.

The period of the late teens is a time when a person is most concerned with the great social and moral issues, and is most ready to reach conclusions that are socially and ethically desirable, not limited by selfish and material considerations. It is a period of idealism, of concern for social justice, of readiness to ask questions about the ultimate meanings and purposes of life. The church can help young people to follow their ideals in an intellectually disciplined way to conclusions about major social problems and personal decisions.

5. *Achieving Intimacy.* In early adulthood one of the dominant concerns is to learn to share life intimately with others and especially with a partner of the opposite sex. This is the psychological basis for family life. There is probably less the church can do to help the individual with this task than with others. However, marital counseling has a bearing on this task, and anything the church can do to bring young people together in situations where they can learn the arts of friendship will help young people approach this task with greater assurance of success.

6. *Exercising Responsible Parenthood.* During the period of early adulthood there are several parallel dominant psychosocial tasks. For the persons who marry and have children, the task of exercising responsible parenthood soon becomes so engrossing that it occupies most of the attention of mothers and much of the attention of fathers. This task extends for twenty-five to thirty years for most people, starting with the first child and continuing until the last child is grown up enough to be independent. It commences with the lessons of rearing young children

and ends with those of setting adolescent children free. So important is parental care of children to their moral development that most churches give a great deal of attention to instructing parents in the art of raising children. Of the many tasks of adult development, this one gets more attention from the church than any other.

Personality Development and the Adult Psychosocial Tasks. In helping adults with their developmental tasks, the work of the church should be related to what is known about personality development during the adult years. Personality does develop, and in directions that are sufficiently common to various people to serve as a basis for planning educational work with people in different decades of adult life. We will use the terminology of ego-psychology, with a definition of the ego as those processes concerned with relating the self to the environment; with the growth of competence; with selection, regulation, and integration of behavior; and with the control of outcomes.[19]

The ego, thus defined, changes during adult life, but the *basic personality* does not change very much. The basic personality is the structure of deep-lying drives and attitudes, largely unconscious, which seems to be rather firmly established during the early years of life. The ego is related to the basic personality, but is more affected by the individual person's experience in life and is always more or less open to development.

On the whole, it appears that the ego expands and becomes more outgoing during the first half of adulthood, from about twenty to about forty-five, and then contracts and becomes more inwardly turned and more self-concerned during the latter half of adult life. This set of changes is described by Neugarten as follows:

> In the broadest and most sweeping terms, the development of the ego is, for the first two-thirds of the life span, outward toward the environment; for the last part of the life span, inward toward the self. To elaborate, in these impressionistic terms: it is as if the ego, in childhood, is focused upon the development of physical, mental, and emotional tools with which to deal with both the inner and the outer

worlds, and with which to carry on its transactions with the environment. In young adulthood, the thrust is toward the outer world, and toward mastery of the environment. In middle age, there comes a realignment and restructuring of ego processes; and, to the extent to which these processes become conscious, a re-examination of the self. In old age, there is a turning inward, a withdrawal of investment from the outer world, and a new preoccupation with the inner world. Finally, there is a stage in which the ego undergoes something of a last restructuring preparatory to death.[20]

With this in mind, one can look at the remaining psychosocial tasks with the understanding that people in their forties are generally more active and outgoing than people in their fifties and later. Forty-year-olds see their world as rewarding boldness and risk-taking. Then, as they grow through the fifties, people see the world as more complex, requiring carefully thought out strategies for the solution of social problems. They see themselves less as forceful manipulators of the world and more as thoughtful persons whose analysis of the world may lead to improvement.

7. *Becoming a Productive Worker.* With its great stress on material welfare, our society impresses upon everyone the importance of the task of working productively. And since the financial and prestige rewards are scaled to a hierarchy of positions in the working force, most persons want to improve their effectiveness as workers. Therefore they try to increase their skill and knowledge, and they seek promotion. How is this connected to the teachings of the church, if it is connected at all?

The various religious groups have various answers. Some are so otherworldly that they regard occupational success almost as evil, or at least as unrelated to religion. At the other extreme are some Protestant churches that regard hard work as a religious virtue. A certain minister of the gospel, after his retirement at the age of sixty-seven from a long and effective ministry, felt so guilty over his inactivity that he secured a pastorate in a small country church that could not afford to pay a full-time minister, and he worked for another ten years, until he was somehow certain that he had done his religious duty. "I could not face my

Maker," he said, " if I was not sure that I had worked conscientiously all my life."

The church does teach an attitude toward work, formally and informally. In fact, the church may find that it is overdoing this kind of teaching for the coming " affluent society." As our society solves the problem of producing enough goods for all its people and then has a surplus, some of the attitudes that go with productivity may have to be changed; for instance, the attitude that a person who does not work is unworthy. This deeply entrenched Christian attitude tends to make a Christian look down upon a person who cannot find a job in a society that does not have jobs for all its adult members.

Recently, an economist stated the proposition that the United States should guarantee everyone an adequate income, whether he works for it or not. The economic reason for this is that an adequate income is necessary for everybody so as to increase the demands for goods and services and thus maintain a fairly high degree of employment and productivity in the society. But some people were morally shocked at this proposal. They claimed that it would encourage laziness, or a " getting something for nothing " attitude, which would undermine the character of the American population.

Whatever one may think of this particular proposal, it appears that an affluent society must reconsider some of its values and decide what value work should have, and how employment, if there is not enough to go around, should be divided up among people. This is likely to become an ethical problem, on which the church will want to take a position.

Thus the church may find itself involved in teaching people an ethical attitude toward productive work rather different from what it has taught in the past.

8. *Exercising Responsible Citizenship*. Most young people are so much concerned with family and work that they do not have much time and energy left over for active citizenship. However, by the thirties the concern for the broader social welfare shows itself with increasing attention to the social and civic problems

of the local community, the nation, and the world. The earlier ideological thrust of adolescence toward simple and drastic solutions is followed by a more mature and realistic and cautious kind of citizenship. Middle-aged men join civic groups that work on political and economic and social problems. Women join the League of Women Voters and church societies that work for social welfare.

The church can offer modes of expression for people working at this task. The local church may have a social action committee. The women's missionary society may make a serious study of issues in the conduct of foreign missions. Men and women may support the work of the church federation in a big city. The Roman Catholic Church gives opportunity and stimulus for responsible citizenship through its Catholic Action groups, and such societies as that of St. Vincent de Paul. The Jewish temples and synagogues have sisterhoods, Councils of Jewish Women, B'nai B'rith, the Anti-Defamation League, and other organizations to stimulate and channel the civic activities of their members.

9. *Using Practical Wisdom for the Social Welfare.* As people get into their fifties and sixties, they move from *energy* to *wisdom* in their civic activities. They may be fully as much devoted to the welfare of society, and their efforts are fully as important.

The church frequently seeks out men and women in their fifties and sixties for positions of lay leadership. They may serve on church boards and committees, and they may take the lead in forming study groups on problems of the local community or on the great economic and political issues of the day.

The individual man or woman often finds himself with a good deal of free time. He retires from work, or she sends her children out into adult life. This is a good time for a shift of emphasis away from family and work roles toward the role of citizen and of active church worker. The church can help the person at this age to find out how he can best serve society, and often the answer will be through active discipleship in the church.

10. *Disengaging from Active Life with Personal and Social Responsibility*. As people grow past sixty they generally commence to disengage themselves from some of the activities and responsibilities of middle age. Men and women who have led active careers in business or professions commence to reduce their responsibilities and get ready to retire. Women who have led a responsible life as mother and housewife reduce some of their obligations. People who have been officers of civic and social and church organizations relinquish these offices to younger persons.

The fact of disengagement may be accounted for partly by the pressures that society exerts on older people to remove them from positions of responsibility and importance as their energy and alertness begin to decrease, and partly by a desire on the part of people as they grow older to give up some of their more strenuous work and heavy responsibility.

However, disengagement is a difficult process for many people who have invested themselves in their work, their family, their church, and their society in general. They may not want to withdraw their investments of energy and ego-involvement. Even though they recognize the inevitability of disengagement if they live long enough, they postpone the day as long as possible. The average person during the decade from sixty to seventy slowly learns to accept the process of disengagement, and often feels bitter about it. After seventy, this person generally learns to see the advantages of disengagement. The average person during his sixties needs to learn how to withdraw or disengage from societal tasks while he retains a sense of personal and social responsibility for the welfare of his society.

The church may assist in this process in several ways. For one thing, the church has positions of trust and usefulness that do not require all the energy and action of middle age, and the church can award these posts to older people. Also, the church can welcome older people to the mixed-age groups of women and men that meet during the week. Older people can be made welcome in the church family, so to speak. The church may also organize a senior group for those of its members who have accepted disengagement and prefer to associate with their own age-mates in social activities that are less demanding than those of mixed groups — that meet during the daytime rather than at night.

Disengagement from the tasks of middle age may be thought of as a redistribution of energies and ego-investments, with a higher level of engagement in family and friendship and church activities, while there is a decrease of engagement in economic and wider community activities.

Finally, there comes the end of life. Whether this comes unexpectedly and suddenly, or is a slow and conscious process, it is somehow the culmination of one's life. Death is difficult for some people, and easy for others.

People who are moving successfully through the process of disengagement with a full sense of personal and social responsibility say they do not fear death. They have a sense of fulfillment. They have lived their lives fully and with competence and dignity.

The church has helped them more by what it has done for them during their lives than by what it does for them at the last moment, however important the last ritual may be to them.

Conclusion

Through the adult part of the life cycle the church does the following things for its members:

1. Encourages and teaches and provides an institutional setting for the ethical performance of certain developmental tasks, especially those of citizenship, work, and family life.

2. Gives specifically religious teaching in terms of concepts and experiences that appeal to adults rather than to children and adolescents.

3. Through its fellowship of religious love, continually supports its adult members as they seek to perform their developmental tasks in ways that accord with their religious ideals.

Through the entire life cycle the church accompanies a person on his journey. The church makes a contribution to *competent* living at every age. It helps to give an *ethical* quality to the achievement of developmental tasks. Finally, the church helps to give a *spiritual* quality to the achievement of developmental tasks.

III. THE CHURCH AND MORAL CHARACTER: WHAT AND HOW TO TEACH

The great living religions have systems of ethics attached to them. They are concerned with the relation of man to man as well as the relation of man to God. Ethics form an essential part of the Judeo-Christian religion.

Furthermore, the Judeo-Christian religion is one that emphasizes individual moral responsibility. Therefore, the transmission of religion involves the teaching of the ethical system to the individual member of the group and depends on his behaving in accordance with the ethical principles he has learned.

In spite of the emphasis that most religions place on ethical behavior, the influence of religion on ethical behavior is problematic. Until the twentieth century, probably more men were killed in religious wars than in all other wars put together. Often the profession of one or another belief about theology was regarded as more desirable than the following of the Ten Commandments. Theological rectitude is often regarded as more desirable than ethical behavior. Unethical behavior has often been excused on religious grounds. The term " pharisee " has become an epithet to be used in describing a religious hypocrite. Highly religious men have practiced evil or condoned it.

Yet being a religious person forces one to be concerned with ethical behavior. Man's incessant wrestling match with sin is a major theme of religious history. Whatever we may say about the success of the religions of the Western world in producing ethical behavior, we know they have tried. Probably a large part of their difficulty is due to failure to understand how moral behavior is produced.

To teach an ethical system, there must be at least an implicit theory of moral development, on which the teaching method is based. In this chapter such a theory will be outlined, which is derived from modern psychology. Each of the various church groups in the United States would probably accept this theory up to a certain point, some going farther than others.

This theory leads to several possible programs of character education. There is likely to be a difference between religious denominations in the type of character education preferred, because of a preference for one or another emphasis in the theory and perhaps because of a rejection of certain aspects of the theory.

Therefore this chapter will present a description and discussion of programs of character education, seen in relation to the theory of moral development.

Theory of Moral Development

Philosophers, psychologists, and sociologists have all been concerned with the "moralization" of the individual by his society. They agree that the human infant comes into the world as an amoral being, endowed with the capacity for moral learning and moral development. He learns to become a moral being through a combination of five general kinds of experience.

Reward and Punishment. Most of the time we learn to repeat behavior we are rewarded for, and to avoid behavior we are punished for. When a baby touches a hot steam radiator he suffers pain, and thus learns to avoid the radiator. He was punished for touching the radiator. Punishment is any experience that brings physical or mental discomfort. When the baby's hand is slapped, or his mother turns away from him and leaves him alone in a room, he experiences punishment, and he tends to avoid the behavior that immediately preceded the punishment. At the same time that he was punished, his mother probably said to him, "Bad boy" or, "Naughty girl," and so he puts punishment and badness together in his mind. Similarly, he puts reward and goodness together. His mother picks him up and hugs him, or she feeds him when he does what she wants him to do, and at the same time she says, "Good boy" or, "Nice girl."

Thus the young child learns what is good and what is bad, and he learns that he will be rewarded for doing what is good and punished for doing what is bad. The young child, however, soon learns that some things that bring him pleasure are not good, but are bad. Touching and throwing certain objects in the house, soiling himself and playing with his excrement, banging on the floor with a doll, and many other things are pleasing to him until he is punished for them. Thus he learns that pleasure is not a sure guide to what is right. Some things are good even though they do not bring pleasure. Other things that bring pleasure will be followed by punishment and are bad.

The essential thing about this early training is that it is directed toward the control of impulses. At first the young child is a pure sensory-motor organism, until he learns to inhibit some of his impulses — to refrain from crying, eliminating body wastes at inappropriate times, striking people. He learns to inhibit certain impulses because he is rewarded for doing so by his mother's love or by other things he has come to value, or because he is punished for impulsive behavior.

Beyond the family there are other agents for teaching moral behavior. Teachers, age-mates, neighbors, employers, and eventually people whom a person does not know individually exert a rewarding or punishing influence upon him for things he does or does not do as he goes through life. They do this mainly through expressing approval or disapproval of his behavior.

Besides the human agents of reward and punishment there are supernatural ones. In some of the simple preliterate societies there are supernatural "beings" who appear physically to punish or reward children for their behavior. Thus, in the Hopi and other Pueblo Indian tribes there are periodic visits by kachinas — young men who are masked and dressed in a special costume as supernatural ones — who come every few months to whip the bad children and to give toys and sweets to the good children.

Another form of supernatural punishment is "immanent justice," a process by which the unseen forces that pervade the world can punish a wrongdoer. He will have an accident or bad luck if he does something wrong, even though he is not seen doing it by any living person. For example, the following story was told to American Indian children of the Southwest: "A boy was out in the fields one day, and he stole a melon and ate it. Later that day he was chopping wood, and the ax slipped and cut his foot." Many of the Indian children said that the ax cut his foot because he stole the melon, and that he would not have been harmed if he had not stolen the melon.

The punishment or reward does not always follow immediately upon the behavior. Rewards and punishments are sometimes received long after the event for which they are given. This is not effective as a teaching device with very young children, who are not able to connect the act of behavior in their minds with the reward or punishment. However, as a child grows up, he becomes able to anticipate reward or punishment in the future from present behavior, though in general such sanctions are less effective than those which follow behavior immediately.

The extreme case of future reward or punishment from present behavior is the promise of heaven or hell in the future life. In order to serve as a control over present behavior, the future reward or punishment would need to be imagined vividly. Some preachers of hellfire probably have succeeded in causing children and young people to curb their immoral acts through fear of punishment in the afterlife. To a limited extent, the Day of Judgment has probably served as an extension of human punishment and reward, if not as a substitute, in the development of moral character.

Modeling or Imitation. A process of unconscious or conscious imitation of another person is now seen as the basis for the learning of a large part of moral behavior, as well as other forms of behavior.

Probably during the second, third, and fourth years of life a child learns to imitate people who are important to him — his mother and father, and older brothers and sisters, at first. He learns this through being rewarded when he models his behavior on theirs. At first his imitative behavior is accidental, but since it is rewarded while other forms of behavior are not so frequently rewarded he gets into the habit of " following in the footsteps " of significant persons. This habit is deeply ingrained and unconscious.

A variety of experiments have demonstrated that with children as young as five or six years a person, even a stranger, who appears to them to be master of a situation (because he is rewarded or people follow his orders, etc.) is taken by them as a model, and they imitate him.

Thus the young child learns to imitate persons who are near and dear to him (significant persons) and persons who appear to him to be successful and powerful.

This behavior is sometimes called role-taking. A child, almost as soon as he can talk, shows evidence of seeing himself as other people. The little girl plays with a doll and says, " I'm mommy." She really means that she believes she is her mother. She will go through life doing some of the things she has seen her mother do because she carries the conviction, deep and unspoken as she grows older, that she *is* her mother. She will also identify herself less deeply with other people she loves or admires — with her father, teachers, friends, movie stars, and later on with her husband.

(The concept of *identification* will not be used as a key concept in this discussion, because it is not necessary to account for the internalization of moral rules and of values, nor is it necessary in accounting for the development of the moral conscience. *Internalization* and *conscience* are key concepts. Psychologists are divided concerning the meaning of the term " identification " and over the evidence for its existence.)

Modeling is a term used to mean a process of acquiring behavior that matches that of another person. It refers both to conscious and to unconscious imitation. By means of modeling, a child can learn a variety of kinds of behavior. He can learn a way of walking or carrying his head or a certain speech mannerism. He can learn moral attitudes and beliefs. He can learn vocational preferences and attitudes toward education.

If parents could wait long enough, they could probably reduce the amount of their moral teaching of children by reward and punishment and do much of this same teaching by example. Children will probably learn table manners by imitating their parents if they are given a chance, but most parents are too impatient for their children to learn these matters to wait for the slower and less painful process of learning by imitation.

Didactic Teaching. The most obvious method of moral learning is through didactic teaching, which is instruction based upon authority, using a series of "Thou shalt" and "Thou shalt not" directives. This method is used by parents, teachers, and clergymen. Its effectiveness probably depends on the answers to the following questions: (1) Is it associated with immediate reward or punishment? (2) Does the teaching come from a powerful or respected person? (3) Does the learner have an attitude of respect for authority?

Although didactic teaching may be usefully combined with reward and punishment or with the example set by a model person, when it stands alone it is probably quite ineffective. A story is told of the ineffectiveness of didactic teaching when not assisted by other forms of teaching, in France, where there is a compulsory course in "moral behavior" taught in the public schools. The lesson on "being kind to animals" is studied by the pupils throughout the French countryside at a certain time of the year. This time happens to coincide with the open season on the hunting of a species of small bird that is much liked by the French people when it is baked in a meat pie. Thus the child comes home from his school lesson on being kind to animals and finds his father returning proudly from a day's hunting with a bag of a dozen birds that the whole family enjoys for dinner that evening.

Social Experience Combined with Cognitive Development. The sheer experience of living with other people and learning to get along with them in a responsible way leads to moral development. A child participates with other children and with adults in a variety of play and work activities. He learns to take many roles in these situations, so as to make the play and the work go along in satisfactory fashion. Thus he acquires a set of rules of responsible moral behavior. All the time he grows in intellectual grasp of the situations in which he moves. He becomes able to define these situations in terms of rights and duties, and of reciprocity, and he develops the ability to see his own behavior from the perspectives of other people.

This aspect of moral development is seen most clearly in the development of children's understanding of and attitudes toward rules of games. Games are important to children. In order to play games they must learn what the rules are. Respect for rules is the essence of morality. Children start to play games, such as the game of marbles, with the idea that rules come from persons in authority, parents or God. Then they gradually learn that rules can be modified by the players so as to make the game more satisfactory, and eventually they come to a stage of rule-making, or morality, by cooperation. Thus they achieve a cooperative or democratic morality, which carries over into other aspects of their lives.

This aspect of moral development has been studied by Piaget and his successors, and has recently been modified and systematized by Kohlberg into a theory that is well supported by experimental evidence.[21]

Moral judgment is a result, then, of cognitive or intellectual development associated with development of a sense of right and wrong. Moral development occurs as the mind develops, but is determined by the kinds of coercion used by parents and other adults, and by the kinds of experience in cooperation with other children that a society provides.

No doubt punishment and reward, as well as modeling, figure in moral development as explained by Piaget, Kohlberg,[22] and others. However, the influence of these elements on character development is effected through a child's living and playing and working with other people while his mind develops and enables him to understand the moral rules he is learning.

Reflective Thinking and Rational Analysis. All the aspects of moral development thus far presented depend upon other people to show the way, or at least to join with the individual in working together toward more mature forms of moral behavior. However, there is one aspect that depends primarily on the individual as an active agent in creating his own moral development.

Everyone who thinks systematically about moral development in the modern, changing society comes to the conclusion that *reason* must enter actively into the process of moral character development in order that a person may become morally effective in such a society.

Reflective thinking may take place whenever a person comes to a fork in the road of his life and must choose to go one way or the other. If he deliberately thinks of the probable consequences of first the one way and then the other, and then chooses the one that seems to offer the better consequences, he is practicing reflective thinking.

In most of these forked-road situations it is possible to follow the lead of some moral authority, such as one's parents or one's pastor. It is also possible to follow one's own first preference for the thing that will give the most immediate satisfaction, such as choosing to go to a movie on a school night rather than to study for tomorrow's lessons. Neither of these ways is wise in our kind of society. Our changing society is continually confronting us with new situations, where the way that looks most immediately pleasant and attractive proves often to be the wrong way when we reflect about the situation.

Consequently, it is wise and good for the individual to take responsibility for making his own choices in many situations where his action will have important moral consequences. Reflective thinking, however, requires practice and needs to be rewarded if it is to become a habit. Therefore, even in this *individual* aspect of moral development the child needs to be aided by his teachers in home and school and church.

Sanctioning Agents in the Process of Moral Development

Moral development is a process that is instigated from outside the individual and continually pushed forward by a variety of sanctions — punishments and rewards. However, as the individual grows up socially, mentally, and morally, he becomes more and more his own sanctioning agent.

There are three types of sanctioning agents, with a particular response for each type. The general response to a sanction invoked by wrongdoing is anxiety. The individual does something bad. If he does not know it is bad, he has no anxiety. But the sanctioning agent punishes him or at least warns him, and he soon learns to be anxious when he does this thing which he now knows to be bad, because he anticipates punishment. He also learns by the same process to anticipate reward when he does something good.

Each sanctioning agent produces its own particular anxiety response in the individual, as follows:

Sanctioning Agent	*Type of Response*
Parents and community agents	Sense of fear or shame
Supernatural agents	Sense of sin
Conscience	Sense of guilt

When a child does something he knows is wrong, he fears punishment from his parents or from others in the community who will judge his behavior. If he does not anticipate severe punishment, he nevertheless is ashamed of himself, and expects some show of disapproval by the people around him who know of his bad behavior. Thus fear shades into shame.

If the child has been taught that the moral order is supported by supernatural agents who will punish or reward in this world or the next, he feels a sense of sin concerning his transgression.

The child generally develops a self-punishing and self-rewarding entity within his personality that is called his conscience. Although the development of conscience depends on the presence of punishing and rewarding people who teach the child what is right and wrong, the conscience eventually operates in the absence of such people, and thus the child carries his own sanctioning agent about with him. When he acts against his conscience, he experiences a sense of guilt.

These types of response to sanctions against wrongdoing shade into each other, but they have some qualitative differences that interest the psychologist and probably are important in the formation of moral character.

The various religions and the various denominations or subgroups within the great religions make somewhat different uses of the three kinds of sanctioning agents. Many simple preliterate societies rely almost entirely on parent and community and supernatural sanctions, with little or no emphasis on conscience. In fact, the conscience seems relatively undeveloped in the people of such societies. On the other hand, conscience has been relatively important in the moral training of the Judeo-Christian religious groups. Among the Protestant denominations conscience has been regarded as especially important in a program of ethical training.

Internalization of Moral Norms or Rules

Central to any theory of moral development is an account of how moral rules or norms are taken in or *internalized* by a child and made to rule his behavior. Psychologists are not all in agreement on the way or ways by which internalization takes place. Furthermore, they differ among themselves on the definition of *internalization*.

In a broad sense, a person is said to have internalized a moral rule if he obeys this rule in the absence of external sanctions (rewards or punishments). Thus a habit is an internalized tendency to behave in a certain way in certain situations. When used in this sense, internalization is simply a case of learning rules and learning them so well that one applies them regularly.

For some psychologists, internalization has a more restricted meaning, limited to the development of conscience.

All students of moral development regard the internalization of moral rules as the key process, and try to find out as much as possible about this process of internalization. There are three different views of how internalization can be produced most effectively by the parents and teachers and others who take part in rearing children. These stress three different techniques of child-training: (1) By direct punishment and reward; (2) by withdrawal of love; (3) by other-oriented techniques, such as reasoning and promoting the development of empathy.

There is substantial evidence from studies of children that the three techniques result in rather different forms of internalization of moral rules.

Direct punishment and reward include physical coercion and assertion of the parent's or teacher's power over the child. This form of training produces fear and shame responses and makes the child sensitive to the probability of being detected and punished by others. The child internalizes a fear of punishment (for bad behavior) and an expectation of reward (for good behavior). But if it seems clear that the behavior will go undetected and therefore unpunished or unrewarded, the child's behavior will not be affected. Thus the internalization has a severely limited power over the child's behavior.

Withdrawal of love takes the form of telling the child that he will lose his parents' love if he does wrong, or of shutting him up in solitary confinement, or of telling him that other children will not like him. When this form of indirect punishment is accompanied by a genuinely affectionate relationship between parent and child, it results in the strengthening of the child's conscience, or the internalization of the parents' or teachers' moral rules in such a way that the child feels guilty over his transgressions and tends to control his behavior even when he is not detected or is not likely to be detected by others.

The other-oriented techniques concentrate on making the child understand that his behavior hurts other people. These techniques require the child's ability to put himself in the position of other people and to empathize with them. The parents start by pointing out to the child how his behavior is harmful to his brothers or sisters, or to other children. In later years, the parents point out to him that his behavior in school, in play groups and elsewhere, reflects on them and makes them feel bad. This method of moral training combines an appeal to the child's reason (he understands the connection between his act and the distress of other people) with an appeal to his sense of empathy (vicarious experience of another's pain). Furthermore, this kind of training generally includes the rewards of parental approval when the child makes restitution (apologizes or does something to help the person he has harmed).

This method of moral training assumes the early appearance of the quality of empathy in the young child. There is evidence that empathy appears quite early in a child's behavior. It does not have to be explicitly inculcated. It is a natural part of the child's behavior repertory. As the child grows older, his capacity for empathy grows into a more sophisticated ability to put himself in the position of others, and the parents or teachers do not have to be so crudely didactic — telling him frequently that he is hurting someone. Instead, they can rely more on the child's conscience to point out to him the harmful consequences of his misbehavior. His capacity for empathy makes him feel guilty when he becomes aware of the harm he is causing to others.

Continual Need for External Support of Internalized Norms. While internalization of moral rules certainly does take place in most people, the effectiveness of the internalized conscience is likely to wear off unless the environment continues to support the moral code that has been established. For example, a child who has been taught that dancing is immoral and then goes as an adolescent to a school or college where "everybody" dances is more likely to change his attitude on dancing than another person with similar upbringing who goes to a school or college where there is a social group available to him which is opposed to dancing.

Continuous external pressure against a person's conscience may reduce the effectiveness of the conscience. For example, a person whose conscience is set against race prejudice may gradually lose this set if he lives in a society that practices racial discrimination (against Jews, Negroes, or any other racial group), provided the society keeps up a steady pressure on him but does not push him to the point where his conscience actively rebels.

Thus the external pressures are effective in altering a person's conscience under certain conditions.

Sequences or Stages of Moral Development

It is natural in the study of a developmental process to think in terms of a series of steps or stages through which the individual passes as he grows more mature. Several attempts have been made to define such a sequence of stages, based on empirical studies of children and adolescents. The following scheme, worked out by Peck and Havighurst,[23] was based on a study of adolescent youth. The authors found five types of moral character or moral motivation, which could be ranked in an order of maturity. However, they did not study a group of people from infancy to adulthood, and consequently they do not have empirical evidence that an individual passes through these types in a sequence of development.

1. *Amoral-Impulsive.* The first stage is characteristic of infancy, when the child is no more than an animal seeking to satisfy his impulses, and having little or no inhibition of impulse. Most children grow through this stage, but a few do not. These few become what is called clinically a "psychopathic personality." Such a person obeys his own impulses, regardless of how this affects other people. These impulses may lead him into delinquency and criminality. If his impulses are friendly, he will be like a friendly animal, and may be known as "charming but irresponsible." He has no conscience and no personal control of himself.

2. *Egocentric-Expedient.* After the first year of life the child learns to inhibit his impulses in order to gain rewards or to avoid punishment. This is the normal condition of the period from age one to age three or four. He is primarily self-centered, but can behave in what society defines as a moral way in order to gain advantages for himself. As a child he learns the value of conforming to the expectations of his family, but he still regards himself as the center of things and will readily do immoral things if he sees an advantage for himself. As an adult this kind of person is always seeking his own satisfactions, but he is smart enough to put up a front of morality. In the long run this person is morally inconsistent.

3. *External-Conforming.* As the child progresses up the age ladder he learns a general principle of conformity, which characterizes him from the age of three or four up to about twelve years. He conforms to the rules of his family, and later to the rules of his peer group. He defines " right " as acting by the rules of behavior that have been laid out for him. He accepts social conformity as good for its own sake, and makes this his principle motive in life. This type of moral motivation may be the characteristic adult motivation in some simple primitive societies where the chief moral sanction is approval or disapproval by the tribe. Such people do not have a strong inner control or conscience. They behave very well according to the mores of their society, unless they are thrown into situations where the rules are not clear or where the prevailing moral standards are bad ones. They take the color of their surroundings.

4. *Irrational-Conscience.* The child usually takes into himself the moral voice of his parents by the age of four or five, and may become a slave to it. He does what his conscience tells him to do, regardless of its effect on other people. Thus, if he has been taught to tell the truth, he may do so in such a rigid way that he hurts other people. He has no flexibility, and cannot readily apply two different moral principles, such as kindness and honesty, in the same situation. An act is " good " or " bad " to him because his conscience tells him so, and not because of its good or bad consequences in his own life and the lives of others. This person is likely to have what is known as " strong " character, and to feel extremely guilty if he does not obey his conscience. He can stand out against the crowd. He can be a martyr. However, in a changing society his rigid conscience may be so strict and explicit in its orders to him that he may do things with bad moral consequences because he is not able to look rationally at the consequences of his behavior and adapt it to serve moral ends.

5. *Rational-Internalized-Altruistic.* At this level a person has an internalized set of moral principles by which he judges and directs his own behavior. But, in contrast to the irrational-conscience type of person, this person has a rational control of himself which permits him to assess the results of his actions in a given

situation, and to approve or disapprove them on the grounds of their actual consequence and not entirely by his own intentions. Thus, if he has assessed the situation inaccurately and finds that his well-intentioned behavior does not produce good consequences, he concludes that he has misapplied his principles and must seek a better application of them. He does not question his principles, but he works rationally to apply his principles so as to produce good effects. On the other hand, the irrational-conscience type is likely to go ahead stubbornly and unimaginatively, doing harm while he is obeying his moral principles.

The rational-internalized-altruistic person is consistently honest, responsible, loyal, kind, etc., because he believes in these principles and sees that they work to everyone's benefit. He is able to accommodate one principle to another — such as honesty to kindness — when they seem to conflict and to require some sort of rational calculation of their consequences in which one or the other principle is given priority. He is not interested in obeying a principle for its own sake, without regard to its human consequences at a given time and place. He has a strong conscience, but he can test, modify, and apply its directives in order to achieve the purposes for which he knows the principle exists.

This person is capable of self-sacrifice and does not hesitate to sacrifice himself if he knows it will genuinely help others, but he does not do so for neurotic self-satisfaction.

A somewhat similar series of stages has been defined by Kohlberg,[24] derived empirically from a study of youth aged ten, thirteen, and sixteen, with also a small group of six-year-olds. He finds that there is an age trend in his stages, though there are many exceptions to this trend. The Kohlberg stages are: (1) punishment and obedience orientation; (2) naïve instrumental hedonism; (3) "good boy" morality of maintaining good relations and seeking the approval of others; (4) authority-maintaining morality; (5) morality of contract and law; (6) morality of individual principles of conscience.

If stages of moral character do exist, moral education should take account of them, with the aim of helping the individual to move through the earlier stages at an appropriate speed, and helping him to avoid fixation at one of the earlier and less mature stages.

Types of Adult Character

Independent of the extent to which research confirms the existence of a developmental sequence in character development, such research does confirm the existence of several types of adult moral character, which are more or less "mature." Four such types are related to the Peck-Havighurst theory and have counterparts in Kohlberg's theory and in the work of Hoffman.[25]

Expedient. The basic motivation of this type of person is to do whatever will give him the most power and pleasure. He can control his impulses if he foresees punishment, but he gives play to his own selfish impulses whenever he sees this as safe. Certain notoriously unprincipled politicians and business and labor leaders belong to this type.

External-Conforming. This type of person controls his behavior in terms of the reward or punishment he thinks it will bring from the society around him. His basic principle of behavior is to conform to social expectations. He has a very weak conscience.

Irrational-Conscience-Controlled. This type of person has a powerful and rigid conscience which controls him. His behavior is conventional in the sense that it conforms rigidly to the rules he has been taught by parents and teachers who were generally punitive toward him and rigid in their own behavior. He will be unconventional if he happens to get into a community or social group with moral attitudes and beliefs different from his own.

Rational-Altruistic-Principled. This type of person keeps his conscience open to reason, and operates on the basis of moral principles which he applies rationally to new situations as they arise. He is particularly responsive to the consequence of his actions for other people. He feels guilty if he becomes aware of harmful consequences of his behavior even when his behavior was based on what seemed to be the best of moral principles. To use psychoanalytic terminology, this person has a strong ego and a positive, confident ego-ideal. On the other hand, the irrational-conscience-controlled person is ruled by a strong superego with many rigid prohibitions.

Alternative Goals in Religious Character Development

Every social group has an implicit set of goals for the character of its members. " A person of good character " can be described with agreement by most members of the group. Every religious group has its own ideal type of moral character.

Of the four types of adult character just described, it is unlikely that any religious group would favor the first — the expedient. But each of the other three would find support and approval from one or another religious group. Even the external-conforming type of character might be regarded as ideal by a religious group in a simple society that has fixed rules to govern every aspect of behavior, and relies heavily on public opinion together with supernatural beings to punish and reward people for misbehavior. Some of the separatist and rural religious sects in a modern society might favor this kind of character. The other two types, the irrational-conscience-controlled and the rational-altruistic-principled, are definitely favored by the moral attitudes and practices of one or another religious group.

It should be mentioned here that both of the more mature types of character imply the existence of moral principles of absolute value. Neither is relativistic. The difference between the two in this respect is that the principles are interpreted and applied rigidly in the case of the irrational-conscience type, while the rational-altruistic-principled type interprets and applies principles in such a way that the rationally foreseen outcomes of behavior are used to test the applicability of the principle.

How the Church Teaches Character

The foregoing description of the development of moral character makes clear why the church has relatively little direct influence upon moral character. The family is the first and the most effective moral teacher. The school can conceivably have some influence upon moral character if it works consciously and systematically at the task.

The weekly Sunday school lesson is a feeble instrument, with its didactic teaching often given by teachers who have little personal appeal as models to the pupils and are not in a position to reward or punish them effectively. To be really effective, the church should penetrate the lives of its youth with rewards and punishments, or with activities that provide models of moral behavior in the persons of teachers and peer-group leaders, or with exercise in reflective thinking and analysis of the moral consequences of human behavior.

Since very few churches do these things effectively, it is no wonder that the findings of Hartshorne and May [26] have stood unchallenged for thirty years. In the Character Education Inquiry, these researchers found that church membership and church participation had relatively slight relation to moral behavior and moral reputation. The relation that did exist could be largely accounted for by the fact that young people of the lowest character have little or no contact with churches. Havighurst and Taba [27] found that adolescents who rated high on religious activity in church tended to have high character reputations. This does not imply a causal relation between religiosity and character reputation; both may be results of family influence.

One thing the church does for its younger as well as for its adult members is to provide a continuing reinforcement of the internalized moral standards that have been learned in the family and the peer group. The sermons of the pastor and the public opinion of the congregation keep a quiet pressure on the members to measure up to their internalized standards.

The most effective way a church can influence the moral character of its youth is to teach parents about the moral development of children and to suggest the ways by which they should raise their children.

The record of the Union College Character Research Project is an example of the systematic use of the resources available to the church. This program requires a close contact with the family, the development of a strong peer group under the influence of the church, and the commitment by the teacher of a great deal of his time to being with his pupils and to studying them.

What Character Type Does the Church Prefer?

It is likely that the leaders of a given church denomination could state their preference between the two types of " strong " character that have been delineated here — the irrational-conscience and the rational-altruistic-principled types. However, instead of choosing the pure irrational-conscience type to the exclusion of the rational-altruistic-principled, or vice versa, they might define their favored type as a combination of rigid conscience with rational-principled conscience in a certain ratio, so to speak. They would certainly favor internalization of moral norms. They would differ among themselves on the relative importance of the superego and the ego, and they would differ in the importance they ascribed to supernatural sanctions.

If a given church group were to define the kind of moral character it wanted to develop in its youth, and the extent to which it wished to rely upon the various types of sanctioning agents, a scientist could probably help it to devise a moral development program, working through parents, church teachers, and church groups. We know enough about the development of moral character to write a program for the kind of moral character we want; and presumably a church could exert a major influence on the character of its coming generation of members by working out such a program.

A church that wished to develop the rational-altruistic-principled type of person would probably go farther than other churches in the attention given to the moral education of its teenage youth. This would be done because boys and girls would need a great deal of practice in analyzing complex human situations for their moral significance — a kind of practice seldom given within a family or a secular school. The church would need to help young people apply moral principles to the social and political and economic problems of the day. It would need to help them search out the probable moral consequences of their own choices being made by responsible people in the society around them.

On the other hand, a church that favored a strong, conscience-dominated character with close dependence upon authoritative moral and religious principles would aim primarily at instructing its youth as to what is right and what is wrong, and would offer its own external support for behavior conforming to church norms, through youth groups and other social supports.

IV. THE CHURCH AND BROTHERHOOD IN THE METROPOLITAN COMMUNITY: WHAT AND HOW TO TEACH

To think seriously about the church in the world today is to think of it as an urban phenomenon. But the church has grown up in a rural society and is now painfully finding its place in a metropolitan society.

Thinking of the church as an institution striving to work out its mission in contemporary society, a French Catholic, Emmanuel Cardinal Suhard, wrote:

> [The Church] has remained frozen in feudal forms which worked in times past. In our time, instead of being fused with society as she was in the middle ages when the parish and the commune had the same extension and the same life, the church is "absent" from the City. She hovers over humanity instead of being incarnate in its flesh and blood. In her message to men she has everything she needs, even more than she needs, to animate the contemporary structures and to draw up plans for the future, but she does not use her resources. . . . In scientific research, social legislation, or humanism she has few innovations. It is not in this way that she will win the world to Christ.[28]

An American, Gibson Winter, sees the church searching for ways to become effective in the creation of a Christian metropolitan society. With the metropolitan areas fractured into suburban and slum segments without any social unity, he proposes that the church has a new mission.

> The underlying thesis of these considerations is that the world is radically changed; a wholly new relationship of Church to world is called for in our time. This new relationship can be described as the

servanthood of the laity. Here indeed we encounter the real division among Christians today: one group feels that the world has not changed in any fundamental sense and that the churches should go about their work as usual; the other group is convinced that the contemporary world has a new universe of meaning, a radically different social structure and problems peculiar to its own time. If one sides with the former group, the churches need only do better what they have been doing. If one sides with those who claim that the contemporary world is radically different in most major respects, then one is open to consider the servanthood of the laity in this new society.[29]

The church must work out a definition of brotherhood fit for the latter half of the twentieth century. It must teach this to its members, both adult and youth.

Throughout the centuries the church has learned to serve the society that existed, whatever form of society it was. Until quite recently this was largely a rural society.

Rural Social Structure and the Church

The Jewish and the Christian religions grew out of a pastoral society. Their book, the Bible, deals with the lives and the problems of a rural people. As Christianity took root in the Roman Empire it became partially adjusted to city life, but the adjustment was tentative, since the end of the world was expected within the near future. Then, as the Christian religion became fashionable, the Roman Empire declined and for fifteen centuries Christianity was a religion of a rural society. It became part of a conception of life based on daily contact with soil and weather. Its festivals of Easter and Christmas were rural. Even when Paris was the biggest city in the world, in the seventeenth century, its citizens, when out for a walk, could see the windmills of Montmartre and drink goat's milk on the Champs Élysées.

The Christian church was adapted to a rural and to an aristocratic society, where everyone knew his unalterable place. Theologians and moralists evolved a theology and a system of morality suitable for this kind of society. When cities began to grow, in the nineteenth century, they were regarded as centers of evil and corruption. The village was somehow more Christian than the city.

Meanwhile, the Jewish church was adapted to city life in a special and limited way, as the Jews found themselves confined in the ghettos of European cities. It was a religion designed to preserve a closed group and family life.

Of course there was much social, political, and economic change from the fifth to the twentieth century, and the church reflected these changes. The Holy Roman Empire fell apart. Nations arose, and national churches. Capitalism developed in close interaction with Protestantism. The Roman Catholic Church experienced a counterreformation. Protestant sects developed, some of them—such as the Methodists—being related closely to social and economic problems of the industrial revolution. There was never a quiet, unchanging century, but the underlying rural economy and aristocratic social structure conditioned everything that happened in and to the church.

Development of American Churches in Relation to American Society, 1800–1950

The North American society started with churches imported from the European mother countries, but the churches changed as the society changed under the impact of political and economic forces that shaped the young and growing country.

There were four broad streams of social change:

1. A rural society developing into an urban-industrial and affluent society.

2. A plural society of European ethnic groups continually renewed and changed with immigration of new ethnic groups.

3. A minority of African slaves evolving into a substantial and separate group demanding equal opportunity, equal status, and integration.

4. A structure of open social classes with relatively great individual upward mobility.

To the social scientist the panorama of church development

and adaptation in a new and expanding society where church and state were separate is a beautiful illustration of the interdependence of a social institution and the social structure. Every definable social group developed its own kind of church to fit its religious needs.

Protestant Middle-Class Denominations. Most characteristic of the nineteenth century were the Protestant denominations of New England, the South, and the Middle West. They found a central place in the emerging social class structure as strongholds of middle-class morality, thrift, and energy. Some leaned toward the upper class, such as the Protestant Episcopal, Presbyterian, Dutch Reformed, Congregational, and Unitarian churches. Others leaned toward the working class, such as the Methodist, Baptist, and Disciples of Christ churches. The Lutheran churches may be put in an in-between middle-class group, which was also ethnic.

These churches found their strength in the agrarian society of the South and Middle West, but they adapted readily to the growing urbanism of the northern states. As the American society became more prosperous some of these churches moved up the social scale, leaving the lower social classes as a recruiting field for the new Protestant sects.

Protestant Lower-Class and Rural Sects. When the rural sects of Central Europe emigrated to America, they found good land and formed farming communities in most of the states from Pennsylvania to the Rockies. As long as they stayed on the land they maintained their ethnic religious communities. Other indigenous sects sprang up in the nineteenth century in the poorer rural areas of the South and in the Midwestern states that bordered the Ohio River. With a fundamental faith in the revelation of the Bible, with strong outward show of religious emotion, these sects moved into the upper lower classes and grew there as the cities grew, converting many city dwellers and gaining adherents from the urban migration of rural Americans. Thus the Pentecostal groups, the Holiness groups, the Assemblies of God, the Church of God, the Church of the Nazarene, the Seventh-day

Adventists, Jehovah's Witnesses, and other sects have grown during the past hundred years.

Negro Churches. Negro Protestant and Catholic churches grew up in the South and the North after the War Between the States, following a pattern that was set by the middle-class churches and often aided financially by them. But the mass of Negroes were working-class people, and their forms of worship were more like those of the lower-class Protestant sects than those of the middle-class denominations. Some Negroes in the North joined the middle-class white churches, but there developed in the North a parallel set of Negro denominational churches with a less intellectual theology, while the " storefront " sects also prospered, especially in the cities.

Catholic Churches. The Roman Catholic Church generally had an ethnic character that came from the European immigrant group that was strongest in a particular area — Irish, German, Polish, Hungarian, Italian. In the smaller cities and in rural areas the local Catholic church served all ethnic groups in the community, as well as all social classes. Here it came the closest of any church to providing an economic cross section of the population. But in the big cities most of the Catholic parishes served separate nationality or ethnic groups and reflected the social-class differences of those ethnic groups.

Jewish Churches. In somewhat similar fashion to the Catholics, the Jews tended to form synagogues or temples around their main nationality groups — German, Polish, Russian — while the earliest Jewish immigrants from Spain, Holland, and England attended generally the church of highest social status if there was more than one group in the city. With a further division into orthodox, conservative, and reformed churches, the Jews in the big cities worked out various adaptations to the society around them.

Other Religious Groups. Several other religious groups came into existence by origination or by immigration during this hundred and fifty years, among them the Mormon, Greek Orthodox, Christian Scientist, Bahai, Buddhist, and Muslim. Those which came by immigration have remained attached to the nationality groups that brought them to this country. On the other hand, the Mormons created a society of their own on an agricultural base, but have since spread out by emigration from their home state of Utah to become similar in sociological respects to the middle-class Protestant denominations.

Upward Social Mobility of Churches. As the American population became both more urban and more prosperous, several Protestant denominations ascended the social ladder with their members — notably the Methodists, Congregationalists, and Presbyterians. They left behind them a kind of social vacuum, which was filled by fundamentalist sects that served working-class Protestants. These sects in turn became organized as denominations and spread widely and rapidly, especially after the beginning of the current century. Many of their members were rural people who moved into the cities. But these, too, moved up the social ladder. They drew more and more middle-class members. A striking example is the Church of the Nazarene. Another is the Church of God (Anderson, Indiana). This group started as a sect in 1878, one of the "Holiness Churches." Characteristic of this movement was the prohibition of the wearing of neckties (termed "superfluities of naughtiness" from James 1:21). This suited a rural group. But by 1910 the movement was gaining headway in the cities, where neckties were worn as a matter of course. One member of the group was a Pittsburgh banker who was also a lay preacher, and later became a full-time minister. Mr. A. T. Rowe wore a tie on business days, and removed it on Sundays, but at the annual camp meeting in 1910 he and a few other ministers appeared wearing ties. This precipitated a big controversy, which was won by the forces of urbanism. As the Church of God grew in the cities it became more and more like other churches. It began to cooperate in local ministerial associations and to work with interdenominational programs. The church took part, as other churches did, in Christian Family Week, Youth Week, Worldwide Communion Sunday, the World Day of Prayer, and Holy Week. These activities tended to replace revivals and camp meetings. The congregations employed college-trained ministers, put robes on the choir, candles on the altar, and moved from plain white frame buildings into stone Gothic or modern redwood structures. In 1957, 57 percent of the members of the Church of God lived in cities of over 10,000 people, and 41 percent of the churches were in these cities.[30]

Not all sects have been ready and willing to move up the social ladder. This can only be done at the expense of some modification of religious beliefs and practices. One group of sects, characterized at first by a fundamentalist interpretation of the Bible and by belief in the importance of personal conversion, has tended to evolve in the ways indicated in the preceding paragraph. For instance, one of the early sects in this group, the Disciples of Christ, or Campbellites, is now largely middle class and rather liberal in its theology. However, the Pentecostal churches, the Assemblies of God, and the Baptist fundamentalists have remained largely working class in composition, with a huge rural membership.

Another group of sects, those centering around Adventist beliefs, have tended to keep to themselves and therefore not to get into the life of the outside world enough to take part in upward social mobility. The Seventh-day Adventists and the Jehovah's Witnesses fit this category.

Still another group of sects have special religious beliefs that do not stand in the way of worldly success. Some of them are Christian Science, Unity, New Thought, and Theosophy. They tend to recruit members from the middle classes.

The Contemporary Situation. If one casts an eye over the church history of the years between 1800 and 1950, one must be impressed by the way in which organized religion adapted itself to a society that was growing by the addition of people from many lands with diverse religious practices; and to a society that was moving from an agrarian to an urban base, with a high degree of socioeconomic structuring. There was a religious form for every taste.

But 1950 was already the beginning of a new era of metropolitan and industrial development in which a new social structure was to emerge. The years grind away at the church as a social institution. The church must be rebuilt to fit the changing society. Will the church recognize and meet the problems in its new environment?

Urbanization, Contemporary Social Problems, and the Church

When people look back upon the twentieth century, and if they are able to look at a century that was completed without a suicidal war, probably they will speak of two chief characteristics of this century — urbanization and technification.

Urbanization is the process by which people collect in large clusters. Fewer and fewer people live " in the country " or " in small towns," and more and more people live in large agglomerations of population.

" Technification " is a word that denotes the process of using machines and natural resources of energy and materials to maximize production.

Until 1800 the people of even the most powerful and up-to-date societies were mainly engaged in getting food and wood from sea and land — some 80 percent of the working population were tillers of the soil, or sheep and cattle tenders, or fishermen or foresters. The growing technification of society enabled fewer and fewer people to raise more and more food, until, today, some 10 percent of the working force in the U.S.A. produces food and fuel for a high standard of living for all.

The farm, the home, the office, as well as the workshop, have all been technified, and with this process has gone increasing urbanization. Larger and larger proportions of the population have come to live in cities. From 1880 to 1960 the proportion of Americans living in towns and cities of 2,500 people or more increased from 30 percent to 70 percent.

The process of urbanization combined with technification to bring material prosperity on an undreamed-of scale. The average worker found machinery at his disposal that enabled him to double his production per hour between 1909 and 1960 while reducing his workweek from 55 to 40 hours. The average per capita income tripled in real purchasing power between 1900 and 1965. Thus the United States has become "affluent." So have most of the countries of the British Commonwealth and the nations of North Europe.

An affluent society is one that produces more goods and services than it can consume with the arrangements that prevail for the distribution of goods and services. In such a society the average income of people is relatively high, and there is very little desperate poverty of the kind that means starvation, high infant mortality, and squalid housing. However, there is a feeling of poverty on the part of low-income people, as well as a feeling of economic insecurity. The affluent society has not yet abolished the problem of poverty.

Although an affluent, urban, and industrial society has solved fairly well some of the material problems of living, at the same time it is involved in vast problems of human relations and adaptation to social change within the country and on a worldwide scale. These problems are ethical as well as social. The church can hardly stand aside from them. The major ones are:

1. *An Interdependent World*. The welfare of the rich nations is tied up with the welfare of poor nations. Most of the poor nations were colonies until recently, and many of the poor nations consist of colored people. The rich nations generally recognize some responsibility for aid to poor and underdeveloped countries, but they have not yet solved the complex economic and ethical problems of giving help in a manner that enables the receiver to help himself and to retain his self-esteem while he is at the same time able to cooperate as an equal with the giver in making the world a more peaceful and orderly place.

2. *Control of Nature*. Through the sciences of physics and synthetic chemistry men are now able to turn matter into vast quantities of energy, and to make new substances that cure disease, resist corrosion, or otherwise do things that naturally occurring substances do not do. Man has gained a substantial measure of control over nature. Technical developments have created ethical

problems, such as that of the peaceful uses of nuclear energy, and the ethical use of contraceptives.

3. *Overproduction and Unemployment.* With technology and automation increasing material production faster than the society is increasing its consumption, the result is an uncomfortable amount of unemployment. This unemployment hits hardest at young people and at workers with low levels of skill and literacy. How is the production to be distributed, and how is unemployment to be controlled and reduced? Some proposals have been made that sound strange to Americans. "Guarantee every person an adequate income," says one group, "and this will result in greater spending, which means greater demand for goods and services and therefore results in greater employment." Somehow this sounds unethical to many Americans, who believe that people should have to work for their money (unless they inherit it), and that a guaranteed income will make people lazy and undermine the nation's character as well as its economy. This represents an ethical problem which must be solved in the near future.

4. *Population Expansion.* By now nearly everybody is familiar with the brute facts of the worldwide "population explosion." Between 1925 and 1965 the world population went from two to three billion. The fourth billion will be reached in 1985 if growth continues at the present rate, the fifth billion in 1995, and the sixth billion in 2000. While food supply increases faster than population in the United States, it barely keeps up with population increase in some other countries, and is falling behind in others. A population policy must be worked out by large sections of the world in order to keep from starvation. This raises difficult ethical as well as political problems.

5. *Race Relations.* The rising demand by American Negroes for full civil rights and educational opportunities offers an ethical challenge that white Americans are not well prepared for— North or South. The churches, most of which are highly segregated along racial lines, have ahead of them a painful period of

self-examination. They can hardly avoid taking positions on housing and employment policies and legislation.

6. *Urban Renewal.* Since World War II vast sums of federal and local government money have been spent to make the big city more livable and more comfortable for those who work there. Acres of slum dwellings have been torn down, thousands of subsidized low-rent dwellings have been built and rented to poor people, miles of expressways have been laid down to enable suburbanites to get from their homes to their work conveniently. Despite the material gains that have been made, the goals of urban renewal are far from being achieved. To make all parts of the metropolitan area pleasant and attractive places where all kinds of people can live and raise families — this is the goal. The task is one for *social* urban renewal, as well as *physical* renewal. The church may be *the* social institution most fit and most needed to take the lead in social urban renewal.

When the question is asked, Who has taken the lead in working on these socioethical problems of the middle of this century? the answer can only be embarrassing to the church. With some honorable exceptions, the lead has been taken by secular organizations. Some of the exceptions are several recent encyclicals of the pope, Catholic Action groups, the American Friends Service Committee, Unitarian Service Committee, B'nai B'rith, the social action and urban church divisions of several Protestant denominations, and the National Council of the Churches of Christ.

The leadership in working on these problems has been taken by a variety of interest groups, composed of people brought together by their interest in one of these problems. There are such groups as the League of Women Voters, the Council on Foreign Relations, peace organizations, National Committee for a Sane Nuclear Policy, Association of Atomic Scientists, Committee on Economic Development, National Conference of Christians and Jews, Planned Parenthood, and a variety of race relations and housing organizations.

This is the first time in the history of Christendom that the churches have not been at the head of the ethical crusades of the time.

Development of the Modern Great City

In order to understand better how the problems of the big city arise and how the church is related to them, it is useful to trace the development of the modern metropolitan area and to show how the churches have shared in that development.

1. *The Beginning.* It commences with a town that is a small trading center, such as Chicago was in 1840. This center grows over a period of years to be a medium-sized city of twenty-five to fifty thousand.

By this time the city has a fairly well defined structure that is related to the incomes and social statuses of the people who live there. One area is where the well-to-do people live. Sometimes it is called the "country club area" because it is close to the country club to which the "upper crust" of society belong. Another part of the city becomes a slum area, with small, old, run-down houses. There is usually one side of town which is spoken of as "on the wrong side of the railroad tracks," where working people live. Their houses are generally well-kept and the lawns are neat, but it just is the wrong place for people to live who want to move in "the best social circles."

The churches reflect the social stratification that is beginning to take place. The several Protestant churches can be ranked by socially conscious observers. At the top are one or more long-established denominations, such as the Episcopal and the Presbyterian. At the bottom are some more recent denominations, with religious beliefs and practices that are regarded as strange by thet rest of the Protestant denominations. If the date is 1850, these may be Campbellites, or various Baptist sects, with the Methodists drawing people who move a little higher in the hierarchy. If the date is 1950, the lower status churches are the Assemblies of God, the Church of the Nazarene, and various Pentecostal Holiness groups. The Roman Catholics may have just one church which draws people from the whole socioeconomic range.

On the other hand, there may be a second Catholic church, serving a recent immigrant group and lower on the social scale than the first one.

2. *The Structured City.* If the city in Stage I is located in a strategic place with respect to water and railway transportation, raw materials or markets, it attracts large numbers of people who come there to work. Soon it develops industries and grows to be a center of several hundred thousand. By this time the areas near the center of the city become industrialized or their houses deteriorate and their owners move away from the center of the old town. Slum areas develop, while choice residential areas appear on the edges of the growing city. Sometimes these areas are annexed by the city.

During this period the churches separate out into types, with qualities of the areas in which they are located. There is likely to be a First Presbyterian, a First Congregational, a First Baptist, and a First Methodist, located in the " best " part of town or made up of the high-status members, while a group of churches of the same denominations are situated in less favorable sections of the city. At the lower levels of the social structure the fundamentalist sects will be found, together with Protestant denominations that serve immigrant working-class people. The Lutheran churches will show some slight relation to the local socioeconomic structure, but more to the divisions of European Lutheranism and therefore will be related to ethnic groups. The Roman Catholics will have a number of nationality parishes, with the Irish and German parishes generally higher in social status because their members have been longer in this country and have had time to move up the socioeconomic ladder. There may be several Jewish congregations, differentiated by the European ancestry as well as by degrees of orthodoxy. Negro churches develop during this stage if the city has a Negro population. The Negro churches are parallel to the white churches and related to the social structure of the Negro population.

3. *Metropolis and the Suburbs.* By the end of World War I a number of American cities had gone through Stage II and were

moving into Stage III. The most significant thing about Stage III is the appearance of choice suburbs at first strung out along the railway lines that lead into the city. These suburbs are exclusive residential areas, expensive to live in, with gardens around the houses, parks and country clubs and tennis clubs, and with superior schools provided at no greater cost to the taxpayer than in the central city. These suburbs are heavily upper-middle-class with a fringe of upper-class and of lower-middle class residents. Their schools are homogeneous along socioeconomic, racial, and ethnic lines.

Churches in the suburbs at this stage are of two types. If the suburb has a history of being a small town for decades before it became a suburb, its already present churches will expand and be reshaped by the newcomers, who will join the ones of their preference and give them middle-class characteristics. If the suburb is a new community, there will be several upper-middle-class churches started by nuclei of members, and these will grow with the community. In many suburbs a community church will be founded, mainly by Presbyterians and Congregationalists, in which all middle-class Protestants feel at home.

4. *Development of the Metropolitan Complex.* Although the big city grew more complex as it passed through the three stages just described, complexity was piled on complexity during Stage IV, which came after World War II. The essential element of this new complexity was the growth of industry in suburban areas, and the essential instruments were the motor truck and the automobile, using the new expressways.

As the great cities grew and expanded before World War II, their suburbs came to include some small industrial cities that had started as independent cities and then were drawn into the expanding suburban web of the neighboring metropolis. There were Chicago Heights, Harvey, Whiting, and Gary south and east of Chicago; Passaic and Elizabeth outside of New York, and Alameda and Richmond outside of San Francisco.

After the war, light industry began to develop in the suburbs. New plants appeared on former farmlands and began manufacturing electronic equipment, plastics, pharmaceuticals, airplanes, and airplane parts. This in turn pulled workers out from the central city into new working-class suburbs. Here the people were mainly well-paid factory workers and minor white-collar workers, with automobiles that enabled them to travel to work independent of railways and electric and bus lines.

Examples of this type of development are seen in the new suburbs northwest of Chicago, in North Kansas City, in Edwardsville and other suburbs across the Mississippi from St. Louis, in some of the new suburbs of Long Island, and in the northern and southern suburbs of Los Angeles.

At the same time, if there was a substantial Negro population in the metropolitan area, a few Negro working-class suburbs came into existence and other suburbs received a migration of Negroes. This happened especially in Chicago and Detroit. With a large Negro slum area developing in the central city, a Negro working-class suburb had real advantages to many Negroes who had their own cars and could get to work as easily from one place as from another. At the same time, Negro middle-class people were finding their way into middle-class suburbs and into mixed Negro-white middle-class residential areas in the central city.

During this stage there develop a variety of suburban churches, to match the growing complexity and size of the suburban mass. Some fundamentalist Protestant churches appear in working-class suburbs, and some all-Negro churches appear in the new Negro areas. And while new churches spring up in the suburbs, some of the earlier very successful churches of the central city die, as their members move away from them and they do not reach out to the newcomers in their local areas. Often their buildings are sold to groups with different church needs.

The Metropolitan Areas

By 1950 the United States Census had defined a " standard metropolitan area " (SMA) that had become a significant unit of population. By this standard a metropolitan area includes a central city or cluster of cities, and the surrounding area related functionally to the central city. The Census Bureau counts a city of fifty thousand or more as a central city of a standard metropolitan area, and includes the whole county surrounding this city, plus any contiguous county that is economically and socially integrated with the central county. A number of SMA's contain two or more cities, such as Minneapolis–St. Paul, New York–Newark–Jersey City, San Francisco–Oakland–Berkeley–Richmond.

There were 212 metropolitan areas in 1960, with a population of 109 million, or 61 percent of the country's population. They gained 24 percent between 1950 and 1960. However, the central cities gained only 8 percent, while the suburban areas gained 47 percent. In fact, some of the central cities actually lost population. In 1950 there were 225 central cities in the 189 SMA's, and 72 of these lost population during the following ten years, while 153 gained. Four of the five cities with populations of one million or more lost people. Los Angeles was the only gainer. Among cities that lost population were Boston, St. Louis, Detroit, Minneapolis, Washington, Philadelphia, Cleveland, Chicago, Cincinnati, Baltimore, and New York, with losses varying from 3 to 15 percent. While the 225 central cities as a group inched up from fifty-one million in 1950 to fifty-six million in 1960, their suburban areas expanded with almost explosive force from thirty-six million to fifty-three million.

The United States is rapidly becoming a metropolitan country. With about 63 percent of the population living in metropolitan areas today, the present rate of growth will bring this proportion to 65 percent in 1970 and 68 percent in 1980. Meanwhile, the population in places of 2,500 and over will increase from a present 70 percent to 74 percent by 1980.

The Suburban Church. As the suburbs are the rapidly growing places in the metropolitan area, and have been for forty years, the suburban church is the rapidly growing element within the church complex. It is there that the new modernistic buildings are to be seen. The church schools are full. Often there are two preaching services on a Sunday morning, to care for the crowds. The church is a hive of club and committee activity during the week. The so-called " religious revival " in the United States gets its most impressive factual support from the growth of suburban churches.

The reasons why people join churches in the suburbs seem to be similar to their reasons for moving out to the suburbs from the central city. Primarily, the suburb is seen as a good place for family life and for children. People report that they moved to the suburb for the sake of their children, and they report that they joined the church for the sake of their children.

The suburban church reflects this set of interests common to suburban dwellers. Some theologians regard the removal to the suburbs as an escape mechanism, and disapprove it, as the following quotation from Gibson Winter indicates.

> Metropolitan man is drawn . . . to an illusory hope for escape from the responsibility for shaping metropolis. The suburban pattern of metropolitan development is symptomatic of this illusion. Suburbia is the image of escape from public responsibility and retirement into the privacy of one's own garden. There are, of course, many practical reasons for the suburban pattern of development — reasons such as the need for space, the technological improvement in transportation and the struggle to avoid tax responsibilities in large urban areas. Nevertheless, many other patterns of residential development could have arisen in the 1920's and 1930's when this suburban process was emerging. . . . The suburban pattern of development arose as an expression of the American dream — a dream of escape from the oppressive disciplines and massive forces of production, an escape from the public responsibilities of a society whose sheer massiveness had put it beyond the range of comprehension. The suburban development is the illusory vision of escape into small town politics, retreat to the little village of knowing and being known. This pattern of metropolitan development is the major alternative to public responsibility and to the creation of metropolis as a human environment.[31]

The contrast of the church in the inner city with the suburban church is described by Scharlemann as follows:

> Life in the inner city is marked by an almost incredible mobility, creating an atmosphere of calloused indifference to human needs and community responsibility. People live in old apartment buildings or

new housing projects; but they keep themselves sealed off from the needs and interests of others in the same building. A pastor may not go from door to door inviting people to his church services. He is not even permitted in the building unless he has someone to call on by name and with the approval of the individual involved. Often there are rooming houses in the area, occupied by human wrecks. Juvenile delinquency, homosexuality, and adult irresponsibility run rampant here. The programs of the churches located in such a section of the city are devoted less to regular public services and more to pastoral counseling intent on rebuilding lives scarred and marred by vice and moral corruption.

By way of contrast, the church in the suburbs is smug and self-satisfied. Most of its members belong to the same income group. They are deeply involved in community affairs, especially such matters as will improve the lot of their children. The problems of the big city nearby do not really concern them.

Without realizing it, their own yardstick of success is used even to measure the activities of the church. Their pastor must be good at public relations. He must be between thirty-two and forty-eight years of age, a middle-of-the-road man in religion and politics. Of course, the congregation provides a rather beautiful ranch-type home for the pastor and his family. Utilities are paid by the congregation; naturally, there is a car allowance. The Sunday services must not run much beyond an hour in length.[32]

These descriptions of suburban churches apply principally to the churches in the "bedroom suburbs" that have grown most rapidly since World War I. Such suburbs are almost entirely middle class in composition. In writing about the church in this kind of suburb, Gibson Winter chose to title his book, *The Suburban Captivity of the Churches.*

Lower-Class Protestant Churches

Throughout the past forty years of metropolitan development, a group of lower-class or working-class Protestant churches have grown in the big cities. Rural in-migrants have been a good part of their strength, but they have had a substantial evangelistic drive to recruit people already living in the city. Fundamentalist in religious doctrine, with an emotionalism that repels the middle class, these churches are communal rather than associational in nature. The people who make up these churches would be repelled by the rationality of middle-class Protestantism.

There is vigor in these churches. Perhaps they have an essential something that the more rationalist churches lack. Ernst Troeltsch, the church historian, when writing of how a new religion takes roots, may have described this kind of church even though he wrote in the early years of the twentieth century and he wrote about the early Christian movements. He commented that the intellectuals in a society *speculate* about religion, but lack religious vitality.[33]

On the other hand, it is the lower classes which do the really creative work, forming communities on a genuine religious basis. They alone unite imagination and simplicity of feeling with a non-reflective habit of mind, a primitive energy, and an urgent sense of need. On such a foundation alone is it possible to build up an unconditional authoritative faith in a Divine Revelation with simplicity of surrender and unshaken certainty. Only within a fellowship of this kind is there room for those who have a sense of spiritual need, and who have not acquired the habit of intellectual reasoning, which always regards everything from a relative point of view. All great religious movements based on Divine revelation which have created large communities have always issued from circles of this kind.

However, the intellectuals must be brought into the new religion if it is to achieve a wide acceptance.

Inevitably, as the movement develops, the early naïve vital religious content always fuses with all the highest religious forces of the intellectual culture of the day; apart from this fusion faith would be broken by the impact of the cultural environment.

Seymour Lipset suggests that this lower-class form of religion is an alternative for working-class people to some form of political extremism. He cites evidence from Finland and Sweden that communism and religious fundamentalism are alternative possibilities for the working class. "The point here is that rigid fundamentalism and dogmatism are linked to the same underlying characteristics, attitudes, and predispositions which find another outlet in allegiance to extremist political movements. . . . 'The communists and the religious radicals, as for instance, the Pentecostal sects, seem to be competing for the allegiance of the same groups.' "[34]

Catholic Churches and Metropolitan Development. Catholics are more likely to be city dwellers than Protestants are. During the 1950 decade some 80 percent of Catholics were living in cities. The metropolitan changes have affected the Catholic churches, but not as profoundly as they have affected the middle-class Protestant denominations. Suburban Catholic churches have been built to accommodate Catholics who have migrated out from the city, but the strength of the church remains in the central city. However, the central-city church has changed a good deal. For one thing, the rule of parish organization by nationality is slowly weakening, as foreign-language groups such as Italians, Poles, and Hungarians have become Americanized. Second- and third-generation ethnics can and do join the parish that they like, or that is located in their neighborhood, regardless of its dominant nationality. In the big cities where there are scores of Catholic parishes, the " nationality parish " is slowly being replaced by the " territorial parish," which serves people in a given geographical area, regardless of their nationality background.

Fichter,[35] in his study of an urban parish, found that fewer urban-born Catholics than rural-born city migrants are " nuclear parishioners," that is, receive Communion weekly and belong to parish societies. He noted that changes in the Catholic churches illustrate the lessening of *communal* characteristics, so familiar in a rural society and also in the lower-class Protestant sects.

The Catholic church in the city, he found, has seen a decrease of: attendance at church suppers, dances, parish festivals, evening services, etc. At the same time, it has seen an increase of: reception of Communion, the sacrament of penance for both sexes and all ages; adult male attendance at Mass; weekend retreats; Cana conferences; Catholic Action; interracial councils.

One might say there has been a shift from rural to urban types of activity.

Jewish Churches. Jews have moved to the suburbs more recently than Protestants and Catholics. Probably the suburban congregations do not differ greatly from the middle-class congregations of middle-class sections of the central city.

Economic and Racial Segregation in the Metropolitan Area

The evolution of metropolitan areas that has just been described has brought about a dangerous situation for American democracy and a disturbing situation for the church which is working to bring the Kingdom of God to this world.

The source of the problem is the growing economic and racial segregation in the metropolitan area. What does the proposition mean—that there is increasing economic and racial segregation in metropolitan areas?

A person is segregated if he lives and works and plays and worships with other people of his own social group. A middle-class person is segregated if he lives in an area of middle-class homes, goes to a church that is almost entirely middle class in composition, does his shopping in a middle-class district, and associates with friends who are middle class. His children are segregated if they live under these circumstances and attend a school that is almost entirely middle class in composition.

In a small city, there cannot be much segregation. All children will attend the same high school, if they go to public schools, and their elementary school is not likely to be solid middle class or solid working class in composition. In their churches, people are likely to meet and associate with other people from as great a range of social status as the denomination covers.

As the small city grows into a big city and then into a metropolitan area, people of similar income and socioeconomic status tend to live together in areas that grow in size, until they are so large that they include the whole membership of a church, the whole enrollment of a high school, and most of the patrons of a shopping district. Eventually, a big city develops into segments or areas of relatively homogeneous composition in terms of income, nationality, race, and other social characteristics.

The city proper finds itself with many square miles of working-class homes, much of this being substandard housing, other segments of small bungalows or of small two- and three-story apartments, occupied by people in minor office and other white-collar work, and by the better-paid manual workers, and other square miles of larger and newer houses and apartment buildings occupied by people of the upper middle class. The more favored areas are probably on the outskirts of the city or stretched out along lakeshore or riverbanks which add to the attractiveness of the area. The suburbs are generally upper-middle-class areas of great homogeneity, but with a growing number of exceptions since World War II.

Into this pattern of economic stratification and segmentation has come the great migration of rural Negroes into the growing industrial cities. The Negroes have generally been segregated, but in the working-class and the middle-class areas of the metropolitan regions.

Thus the chances of a certain man, woman, or child to live near, or attend school with, or worship with, or sit in a park near, a person of different skin color, income, or nationality have become less since 1940. This is the operational meaning of the basic proposition that —

There has been an increase of economic and racial stratification in the metropolitan areas since 1940. This can be seen quantitatively in Table 1, which presents socioeconomic data for the central city and suburbs of Chicago and for the country as a whole. A socioeconomic ratio has been calculated as a ratio of white-collar to blue-collar workers.[36]

TABLE 1

SOCIOECONOMIC RATIOS OF THE CHICAGO AREA

					Chicago City	
	U.S.A.	Chicago SMA	Chicago City	Chicago Suburbs	White	Nonwhite
1940	.66	.71	.69	.77	.75	.17
1950	.71	.77	.73	.86	.84	.18
1960	.82	.92	.69	1.28	.82	.25

Looking at the socioeconomic ratio (SER) for the U.S.A., we see that this ratio has been increasing since 1940, and especially since 1950. This expresses the fact that the proportion of white-collar jobs in the American economy is increasing while the proportion of blue-collar jobs is decreasing. The SER for the Chicago metropolitan area shows a similar increase, and is higher at all three dates than the SER for the U.S.A. as a whole.

In 1940 the city of Chicago was slightly below the average of the metropolitan area. In 1950, the Chicago city SER had increased from .69 to .73, while the total metropolitan area increased from .71 to .77. Clearly, the suburbs were carrying up the metropolitan area total, for they increased from .77 to .86. The city was lagging. The flight of middle-class people to the suburbs was in full course.

But the decade after 1950 saw changes much greater than those which had occurred previously. The city of Chicago decreased in SER from .73 to .69, while the total SMA increased from .77 to .92, and the suburbs jumped from .86 to 1.28. The central city was decreasing its average socioeconomic level, in the face of a countrywide increase, as well as a sharp increase in the Chicago area suburbs.

The racial aspect of this phenomenon is also seen in Table 1 for the city of Chicago. While the SER of white male workers was going up from .75 to .84 and down to .82 between 1940 and 1960, the SER for nonwhites (almost all Negroes) was increasing very slowly, from .17 to .18 to .25. Since the proportions of nonwhites in Chicago increased from 8.2 percent in 1940 to 22.9 percent in 1960, it was the in-migration of nonwhites with relatively low SER that caused a substantial part of the change in Chicago.

Negro Population Changes in the Big Cities. Since 1920 the proportion of American Negroes who live in the 31 "northern" states has tripled. The decade of greatest growth of Negro population in northern cities was that from 1950 to 1960, as is shown in Table 2.

Through the prevailing patterns of residential segregation in

Table 2

WHITE AND NONWHITE POPULATION TRENDS IN THE BIG CITIES
(Population in thousands)

	1900		*1920*		*1940*		*1950*		*1960*	
	Pop.	Non-white %	Pop.	Non-white %	Pop.	Non-white %	Pop.	Non-white %	Pop.	Non-white %
New York	3437	1.8	5620	2.7	7455	6.1	7892	9.5	7782	14.0
Chicago	1699	1.8	2702	4.1	3397	8.2	3621	13.6	3550	22.9
Philadelphia-Camden	1294	4.8	1824	7.4	1931	13.0	2072	18.2	2003	26.4
Los Angeles-Long Beach	105	2.1	632	2.5	1669	3.9	2221	7.9	2823	12.2
San Francisco-Oakland	410	0.7	723	1.1	937	1.4	1160	7.9	1107	14.3
Detroit	286	1.4	994	4.1	1623	9.2	1850	16.2	1670	28.9
Boston	561	2.1	748	2.2	771	3.1	801	5.0	697	9.1
Pittsburgh	452	3.8	588	6.4	672	9.3	677	12.2	604	16.7
Buffalo	352	0.5	507	0.9	576	3.1	580	6.3	533	13.3
Washington, D.C.	279	31.1	438	25.1	663	28.0	802	35.0	764	53.9
Baltimore	509	15.6	734	14.8	859	19.3	950	23.7	939	34.7
Atlanta	90	39.8	201	31.3	302	34.6	331	36.6	487	38.3
Birmingham	38	43.1	179	39.3	268	40.7	326	39.9	341	39.6
Montgomery	30	56.8	43	45.6	78	44.2	107	39.9	134	35.1

Note: Nonwhite includes Orientals, who are present in noticeable numbers in San Francisco and Los Angeles, but not elsewhere in this list.

the big cities of the North, combined with growing economic stratification of metropolitan areas, there is coming about an American form of apartheid. Present trends of population will lead to an even greater concentration of Negroes in the central cities of the big metropolitan areas. City after city may pass the 50 percent mark in Negro population. Washington has already done so. Unless a practical policy of antisegregation is worked out, Philadelphia, Chicago, Detroit, Cleveland, Baltimore, and St. Louis will do so within twenty-five years. Unless residential and educational segregation are successfully overcome, these cities will become half solid black and half solid white.

The tables illustrate the growth of economic and racial segregation by dwelling place in the metropolitan areas. This results almost inevitably in segregated schools and segregated church organizations.

In the case of the public school the process of segregation is quite simple. It generally goes about as follows: An elementary school ordinarily has a district of twenty-five or thirty city blocks. All the children in this district are expected to attend the local school. Seldom is an exception allowed. Into a particular elementary school area a few Negro families move from neighboring areas. Certain white families feel disturbed and threatened by this, and they quickly move out of the school area. Since there is a growing in-migration of Negroes to the city, they are happy to buy or rent the vacant homes. Within a year the proportion of Negroes to white pupils in the local elementary school grows from 10 to 60 or 70 percent. Up to this point a number of white families have seen the school and the local community become "integrated" with satisfaction, because they believe in the principle of racial integration. But as they see the proportion of Negro children rise and pass 60 or 70 percent they, too, become disturbed, because they do not want their children to attend a school with a large majority of Negro children. Therefore they flee from the local community, their houses are taken by Negro families, and the school becomes 95 to 100 percent Negro.

As this happens in an elementary school area of a large city, similar changes may take place in nearby schools, all of which send their graduates to a particular high school. In many cities, residents of a particular area must attend the high school of that area. Therefore, the high school serving an area with a growing Negro population is likely to go through the same kind of changes that the elementary school just described has experienced. A particular high school may have 10 percent Negro pupils in its first-year class one year, 25 percent the next year, and 50 percent the next. By this time, unless the people living in the high school area organize to stabilize the population at a level of nearly equivalent numbers of whites and Negroes, a kind of panic seizes the white families and they very quickly move out to an area farther from the center of the city or to a suburb, and the high school becomes all or nearly all Negro.

This process has gone on in all the big cities of the northern part of the U.S.A. since the close of World War II. It has gone on because industry and business needed unskilled and semi-skilled workers and sought new workers among the Negroes of the rural South. As long as economic opportunity is better in the urban North than in the rural or urban South, Negroes are likely to move into the northern cities.

Underlying this process of racial segregation is the process of economic segregation that has been going on in big cities for a century. The incoming Negroes are largely poor people with low incomes, and they move into cheap housing in slum areas.

There are ways to reduce or to prevent racial segregation and economic segregation in the Northern cities, but these have not been looked for or worked out until very recent years, when the movement for *social* urban renewal has come alive.

Economic and Racial Segregation in the Churches. The process of segregation in the church is also basically related to patterns of residence, but is different from the school process for two reasons. First, the church has *communal* as well as *associational* characteristics. That is, the church is a fellowship of people who tend to live alike as well as to believe alike. Church members are expected to be friends and associates. Marriage within a church group is strongly favored by many churches.

A local church has church suppers and other social events that bring its members into rather intimate social relationships with one another. Under these circumstances there is a strong tendency for people who feel comfortable with one another to belong to a particular local church. Therefore, people of a given social class or of a limited social class range are likely to be found in a particular local church. Also, if people do not feel comfortable with people of a different race, they are not likely to attend the same church. Therefore, in a big city with a number of local churches of a particular denomination, there is a tendency toward economic and racial stratification in the church.

Secondly, a local area in a city has a number of different church denominations, which are to some extent alternatives for the local residents. This is particularly true among Protestants. If a Methodist does not feel " at home " in the local Methodist church, it is generally easy for him to change to a Presbyterian or Congregationalist or Nazarene church where he finds more people who are " like " himself.

In consequence of these facts, a local church tends to be more highly segregated by economic and racial composition than does a local public school. Only a deliberate policy of economic or racial integration is likely to produce an integrated church. The writer has computed the SER for two city churches that he knows. One is a Protestant church located in a middle-class residential district. The SER is 34 — quite similar to that of a typical church in a middle-class residential suburb. The other is a " storefront " church serving some thirty poor families in a slum district. Here the SER is .07. The following cases illustrate the possibilities in the big-city church.

Wesley Methodist. The Wesley Methodist Church was founded in 1910, in a section of the city that was then the most stylish place to live. Its membership contained some of the leading citizens of the city, which at that time had two million population. The social class composition ranged from upper class to lower middle class, with rather few of the latter, since there were only a few owners of small business or office workers who were Methodist and lived within about a mile of the church. Also, the Second Methodist Church was located a mile and a half away, in a mixed middle-class and working-class area, and this church tended to draw away lower-middle-class people who lived within reach of Wesley Church. About 1945 the Wesley area began to change. Negro population growth had brought a solid Negro area within a half mile of Wesley Church. A few Negroes came to services at Wesley. The Wesley choir, one of the finest in the city, recruited several Negro singers who lived not far away.

About 1950, a few well-to-do Negroes moved into the section near the church, buying some of the fine old houses whose owners were selling as they neared the end of their lives. The leaders of the church at this time deliberately decided to encourage Negro membership, and to create a truly integrated church. The Negro membership grew rapidly, and consisted mainly of middle-class Negroes who could afford to live in the area near the church. Many of the white members continued to attend Wesley, even though some of them had moved from their big houses to apartment buildings a mile or more away. Other white members moved out to the suburbs and joined new churches. Almost none of the children of the members of the 1910 period remained in the Wesley area. Gradually the composition of the area changed until it was two thirds Negro by 1960. The church membership in 1960 was also about two thirds Negro, and the white members were older, on the average, than the Negro members. By 1965 the church membership was 80 percent Negro. The area of the city had become stabilized with a ratio of about 50 percent Negro and 50 percent white, but a considerable number of the whites were Jews or Catholics. It is a question whether Wesley Church will remain integrated. It is a desirable church from the point of view of Negroes, and they hope it will retain its white membership. The white members are loyal to the church and they believe in integration, but they are uncomfortable at being in the minority in the church.

The Swedish Lutheran Church. There was a large immigration of Swedes into the city between 1890 and 1905, and they settled in an area of several square miles northwest of the center of the city. Other immigrant groups were in the same area, but there were enough Swedes to support a substantial church which was built in 1900. At first the sermons were given in the Swedish language, but by 1920 the sermons were normally given in English. The Swedes were mostly factory workers or skilled craftsmen, and they prospered, sending their children through high school. The children moved into business and professional work in many cases, but remained to live near their parents, and to attend the same church. The church was strong and thriving in 1930. By 1940, however, this section of the city was changing. A number of rural white immigrants from the southern part of the country were coming to live in this area. Many of the second-generation Swedish people were moving out to the growing edge of the city. While some of them came back on Sundays to church, others did not. Immediately after World War II the changes proceeded even more rapidly, and the congregation became smaller. Almost all of the original immigrant group were dead. The church was finally closed, and the building sold to a congregation known as the Northwest Bible Church. The members of this church were nearly all factory workers, with a sprinkling of people in minor business occupations. They did not live close together, but came from as far as two or three miles to church. Immediately around the church and extending for a mile in all directions was an area of low-rent single-family and six-flat tenements that had become crowded with large families of southern whites, Puerto Ricans, Italians, Greeks, and Poles. Although quite heterogeneous in church affiliation, this area was a solid low-income and slum region of the city.

Holy Cross Church. When Holy Cross Church was built in 1850, it served the entire city. Forty years later there were ten parish churches and the new Holy Cross Church was built on the west side of the city, in an area with a mixture of ethnic and social class groups. This was the nearest to a cross section of the population that could be found in any part of the city. There were many Irish Catholics living on the west side, and they gave the church its special character. From 1890 to 1945, Holy Cross continued to serve a large parish with many different kinds of people of varied economic status. Most of the Irish politicians lived in the area and went to Holy Cross Church. During this period there was a gradual decrease in the average socioeconomic status of the parishioners, reflecting a decrease in the socioeconomic level of the area. A number of Mexicans moved into the area, and a number of Italians. The parish church welcomed these people to church and to the parish school.

After World War II a few Negroes moved into the area, coming from just north of the parish area, where they had a large segregated dwelling area. At first the church was hardly affected, since none of the Negroes were Catholics. But then a number of Negro middle-class families moved into the area, some of whom were Catholics. They went as a matter of course to Holy Cross Church, where they were welcomed. As more Negroes moved into the area, the parish priest began to pay special attention to converting Negroes. He secured a Negro curate as an assistant and began to build up the Negro attendance at the parish school. By 1965 the area was entirely Negro in composition and Holy Cross was a Negro parish.

Congregation Beth Israel. The sons and daughters of Jewish immigrants from Poland and Russia founded Congregation Beth Israel in the 1920's. They had mostly been reared in an area just north of the center of the city, where their parents had settled and prospered. The second generation moved into an area of middle-class apartment houses that were being built after World War I. Here they built their church, raised their children, and sent them to their own Hebrew school after the public school hours on weekdays. For twenty years the Jewish community grew and prospered in this area. Then two things happened to weaken their congregation. A suburb in the fashionable River Forest section of the metropolitan area became open to Jews, who up to that time had encountered insuperable obstacles to buying or renting houses in the suburbs. A considerable proportion of the young adults in the congregation moved to River Forest during World War II and immediately afterward. At the same time, a growing Negro middle class moved into the former Jewish area from a contiguous area of Negro residences. By 1960 the area around the temple had about 60 percent Negroes. The Congregation Beth Israel had declined in numbers, and had very few children to use the educational plant. The members of the Congregation decided to abandon their temple and to enter one or the other of two Jewish temples that were farther out from the city center but contiguous to the district of Congregation Beth Israel.

The decision to abandon their own building and educational plant meant that the property had to be sold. After some search for buyers who could make good use of the plant, the offer of the Black Muslims was accepted. This group of Negroes was growing, and it needed a building for its mosque as well as a school building, since it did not want to send its children to the public schools.

The City Church and Ecological Forces. In all four of the cases just described, the church was caught up and changed by the informal forces of city growth and change. The church building alone remained fixed, but the people in the church and the quality of the church changed. The forces of economic and racial segregation made pawns of the churches. Only in the case of Wesley Methodist was there a deliberate attempt by people to control and direct the forces of population change. Leaders in Wesley Church helped to determine the local community's policy of creating a racially integrated community, and they stayed in the church, often at some sacrifice of convenience, in order to make it an integrated church.

The attitudes of these people are now spreading to other churches in big cities. Church people are talking more and more of working through the church to prevent or reduce the degree of economic and racial segregation in the big cities.

The Negro Revolt. The great moral problem of the churches during the 1960's is the problem of justice and equality for the

Negroes of the United States. Public recognition of their problem has been forced by the so-called Negro Revolt — the movement of Negroes both in the North and the South to seek their civil and political rights and to work for racially integrated social institutions. Though many churches dominated by white people have given official and public support for the Negro cause of civil rights, very few local congregations have become integrated. Local churches are probably more segregated than any other institution in American society. If we should define an "integrated" congregation as one with 10 to 90 percent of white members, the number of Negroes belonging to such churches would be very, very small.

It is easy to understand why church congregations are racially segregated. The communal or fellowship aspect of the church tends to make for racial segregation in a society with prejudice about skin color. Then, too, the historical fact of segregation has given rise to large and strong Negro church denominations, and these have a tendency to resist movement toward integration.

One of the urgent tasks of the church today is to study the problems of racial and of economic segregation so as to understand these phenomena, and then deliberately to work to change the situation.

The Church and Community Problems

As the church confronts the problems of urban community life, it faces a test of its ability to work for the Kingdom of God, and also of its system of religious education. For effective ethical action on community problems requires an understanding of our urban society, which the church should teach to its members. The following are some of the questions that urgently require answers:

Can the urban church meet the problems of metropolitan stratification and of conflict between suburbs and central city?

Can the urban church accept and support the Negro Revolt?

Can the urban church do anything constructive about the youth problems in a big city?

Can the urban church become a mixed social class and mixed racial church?

Can the urban church devise and teach a policy and program of metropolitan planning and urban renewal?

The answers to these questions will determine which of the following visions of the future metropolitan area will be correct.

The Two Visions of the Future Metropolis

Most churches are working to bring the Kingdom of God to this earth. As science and technology have shown the way to an affluent society, the churches have been looking for the ethical way to use this real or potential affluence to improve the quality of brotherhood.

To accomplish this task of applying religious ethics to the existent and emergent society it is necessary to look ahead — to get a vision of what can be and of what is desirable — and then to work toward this goal.

From facts now known about a modern society and from trends now visible it is possible to see ahead fairly clearly for twenty-five years. One can look at a present-day metropolitan area and foretell the size of its population, the income levels of the people, and their racial composition. By studying past trends one can project into the future and prophesy such things as the distribution of people between suburbs and the central city, the relations between income and where people live, the living space occupied by people of different races.

The vision of the future depends on two quite different qualities of a person. It depends on what a person has been trained to see: that is, upon his knowledge of society and its trends. It also depends on his conceptions of human behavior, human motives, and of the effectiveness of such social institutions as the church and the school, which have goals of human betterment.

One kind of person is trained to see the future as determined by the past. He does not expect drastic changes of direction in history, and much less does he expect reversals of the processes he has studied. He may not like what he sees ahead, but he reports it, nevertheless, and he plans on it as a hard reality. This kind of prophecy may be called a *past-determined vision.*

The other personal quality that determines what a man sees in the future is an ethical quality. It consists of ideals, the faith in God and man to achieve ideals, and the conviction that human society can and must be improved. The person with such a quality may have the knowledge of the social scientist. He may know the past and he may understand how past events can be projected into future trends. On the basis of his scientific knowledge he may be able to plan for future action so as to translate his ideals into action. His prophecy may be called an *ethics-determined vision.*

Both visions see some things the same as they look ahead at the next twenty-five years of the metropolitan areas of the country. They see certain things coming to pass uniformly in New York, Boston, Philadelphia, Baltimore, Washington, Cleveland, Detroit, Chicago, St. Louis, San Francisco, and Los Angeles.

They see the population of the metropolitan areas growing rapidly and almost entirely in the suburbs, with the population of the central city remaining nearly constant in numbers. They see the proportion of Negroes increasing during the next twenty-five years, though not as rapidly as this population increased between 1950 and 1960.

Where they differ is in their view of the distribution of people by race and income through the various parts of the area and in the churches and schools.

The Past-determined Vision. Assuming that the future will be like the past, the central city in 1990 has become a collection of working-class communities, separated from one another by motor freight and railway yards, factories, warehouses, and parks, and connected with one another by expressways. Housing is up-to-date and in fairly good condition, with some areas of single family dwellings, some of row houses, and blocks of low-rise and high-rise apartment buildings. Public-supported low-cost housing has replaced most of the worst slums of the 1950's and 1960's.

The exception to the rule that the central city is inhabited largely by working-class people is found in a few small areas of upper-middle-class and luxury housing, some near the center of the city, some stretched out along parks, lakes, and rivers, and some near universities and research institutes.

The central city is about evenly divided between whites and Negroes, with Puerto Ricans and Mexicans and other Latin-speaking groups having substantial settlements in several of the cities. The Negroes and whites are generally quite sharply separated by parks, express highways, railroad yards, and other natural barriers. There is very little residential integration.

By far the largest numbers of schools and churches are practically all white or all Negro. There are even community colleges, teachers colleges, and theological schools that are all white or all Negro. Yet the business offices and the large department stores downtown have a mixture of white and Negro patrons and employees. The city council is evenly balanced between Negro and white aldermen, and the school board has an even balance, while the city public schools have a clear majority of Negro students.

Between some of the Negro and white residential areas there are areas called "transitional," in which white and colored people live. The term "transitional" has several connotations. One is that the area is in process of transition to a Negro residential quarter, to meet the residential needs of the growing Negro population. Another connotation is that the culture of the area is different from that on either side. The people live a bohemian life. There are numbers of interracial married couples. There are numbers of light-skinned Negroes who are getting ready to "pass" into an all-white zone. There also are a few areas of stable integrated housing, where Negroes and whites deliberately choose to live because they prefer integrated schools, churches, libraries, and other forms of association.

In the suburbs there are numerous middle-class communities without Negroes. There are also a few small middle-class areas inhabited almost entirely by Negroes. Several of the industrialized suburbs are small replicas of the central city. They have Negro areas and white areas, with schools and churches serving the different areas separately. There are also several all-Negro working-class communities with their own school districts, and a larger number of white working-class communities. Somewhat less than 10 percent of suburban residents are Negroes.

The distinction between the past-determined and the ethics-determined vision is that the latter depends on a rational effort to direct history in the service of human and religious values, whereas the former assumes that history is determined by blind impersonal forces. There is much reason to believe that great cities can grow in various patterns. The American pattern has not been followed by Paris or by London. Men have a choice in the matter if they are wise enough and determined to make the city serve their ethical purposes.

The Ethics-determined Vision. The metropolitan community since 1965 has made a thorough study of its problems with the aid of specialists in political science and city-planning. Leaders in the planning movement have been representatives of the churches, the professions, business, manufacturing, and organized labor. After several years of study the leaders organized a year of intensive discussion and study by the citizens of the area, in churches, educational agencies, and wherever people could gather for this purpose. Proposals put forward by the commission that had studied the future development of the metropolitan area were debated vigorously, and eventually most of these proposals were adopted by voters or by local governing bodies.

The central action was to form a metropolitan area governing authority, with broad coordinating and planning powers, and with taxing powers that effectively equalized taxes for schools and for municipal services throughout the whole area. This metropolitan authority coordinates the local government bodies such as the city and village councils that have been in existence a long time.

During the twenty-five years since 1965 there have emerged a set of well-defined local communities varying in size from ten thousand to three hundred thousand population. The larger ones are segments of the central city, which has been broken up for purposes of decentralized local government.

The larger communities, from fifty thousand up, are fairly close to being cross sections of the metropolitan area population in economic and racial terms. There is no local community with more than 60 percent working-class people or more than 50 percent Negroes. Negroes make up 20 to 30 percent of the total metropolitan population.

The local community governments came into existence as a result of decisions made by community councils and other organizations that this form of government was best for a metropolitan area. Boundaries of the local communities were determined by study and discussion over a period of several years between the metropolitan area planning commission and local organizations made up of community leaders. Certain broad principles were stated and agreed upon in the early phase of the reorganization. One principle was that each area should be something of a cross section of the population in racial and economic terms. It was assumed and understood that there would probably be some residential and income stratification within a local community. Such a community would have its choice residential areas, and its other sections of smaller or poorer houses. But all people in the community use the same library, the same high school and community college, the same local business section. The churches have become more nearly cross sections of the population in the past twenty-five years, though there are still a few segregated Negro churches, and a few churches that appeal almost entirely to working-class people.

In each local community there is a community council consisting of representatives of the churches, parent-teacher organizations, business and civic organizations. The council makes recurrent studies of the community and uses its influence to get policies put into practice that raise the cultural level of the community and at the same time promote economic and racial integration.

The overall physical structure of the metropolitan area has been worked out by the metropolitan governmental authority to develop into a set of local communities tied together by a network of expressways, but separated by parks and other recreational areas, and by industrial districts. All local communities have fast and easy access to the central district of the city, with its modern business and civic buildings that house the economic and cultural activity which should be available to all people in the area and which cannot be duplicated in the local areas — such institutions as central banks, meeting places for conventions, theaters and museums and orchestra halls.

The dozen great metropolitan areas of the country each have their own physical structure determined partly by the natural features of waterways, hills, and plains; partly by tradition; and partly by a grand city plan developed by architects of cities working with the planning commission to produce a unique structure for each big city.

Ethical Aspects of Urban Renewal. These two visions are two ways of conceiving the course of urban renewal during the next twenty-five years. The big cities are in the process of renewing themselves. They must do this in order to be able to grow as they must and to accommodate people who must live and work together in great cities.

The ethical vision sees the problem of urban renewal as a *social* as well as a *physical* problem. Urban renewal is more than a matter of tearing down old and obsolete buildings, laying out expressways, and facilitating the economic growth of the area. The problem of social urban renewal is one of remaking the metropolitan area so that all kinds of people have a maximum freedom of choice to live and to raise their children in the kind of community they want for themselves.

How the Church May Act in the Metropolitan Area

There are three general patterns that churches adopt in the metropolitan area. Two of them avoid direct involvement in studying and working on the social problems of the big city, in favor of more immediate and limited goals.

1. *The Suburban-Rural Pattern.* Whether located in a suburb, a small city, or in the heart of a big city, this church maintains a

traditional rural character. Its primary goal is to use religion for personal and family comfort. Its moral horizon is bounded by the local community, local school, and local church. Its virtues are orderliness, thrift, individual moral rightness, and conformity to local community mores. What it regards as sins and what it condones are compared by Truman B. Douglass as follows:

> Drinking and carelessness in the observance of sexual conventions — moral divergences which, rightly or not, are considered characteristic of city life — are judged far more harshly than small-town snooping, gossip, Philistinism, and cruelty toward the nonconformist.
>
> The most serious consequence of this moralism is that it makes church people unable to see the real nature of city life clearly and to share in its triumphs. One would expect every Christian to rejoice in the transition of a one-class city neighborhood to a multiracial, multicultural community. Instead city churches usually regard such a development as a serious setback to the Christian enterprise — by which they mean simply that it has made it harder to hew to old ways. They fail completely to appreciate the stunning accomplishment the change represents. It is only in cities that man has begun to cast off the ages-old primitive superstition that the "different" is, of necessity, something to be hated and feared. To be able to walk along Fourteenth Street in New York City or lower Market Street in San Francisco and experience an exultation of spirit at the variety of human features and tongues — and the measure of mutual acceptance evident in the passing crowd — requires a degree of Christian insight and thankfulness not often cultivated in country parishes.[37]

2. *The Urban Middle-Class Associational Church.* In contrast to the type of church that has just been described, there is the associational type of church. Its members belong to the church as they belong to professional, cultural, and leisure-time associations. Thus the church is reduced to one of the groups in which a person associates, with one segment of his personality. He is not part of a church "community" or "fellowship." His personal and moral commitment to the church becomes thin. Robert Lee comments on this type of church as follows:

> With increased specialization of roles and multiple-ministerial staffs in our large urban churches, face-to-face primary group relationships

are weakened, and replaced by associational relationships.

Martin Luther once defined the church as a sustaining fellowship of "mutual conversation and consolation" in which the members love one another and share one another's fortunes and burdens. Yet this is hardly possible in the modern situation in which the church is a part of mass culture. Like its urban ethos, impersonality, anonymity, and mass participation are prevalent in the large urban church. In tune with the rapid pace of urban culture, church members rush to church for a brief hour a week and then are just as quick in leaving its doors. The congregation on a Sunday morning is a sea of more or less impassive faces. Everyone is alone in the crowd, be it subway or sanctuary. Strangers they come and strangers they go.[38]

This kind of church has a middle-class bias, with some severe limitations on it as a means of working for the Kingdom of God. David W. Barry comments on it as follows:

I have been exposed to a good deal of denominational literature in my past and present. It seems to me that there are certain assumptions implicit in this literature about the audience for which it is written. It seems to assume a normative family situation as one with two or three children living in a single-family house with some modest space around it, with a father who comes home at night from working in an office. They live in a community where teachers are pleasant, policemen are friendly, and a fairly decent neighborhood spirit exists. The problems of the children are primarily those of adjustment to other children of like circumstances and learning basic principles of behavior and morality. In the literature they are expected to learn, for example, that Negroes and Italians are children of God and are just as good as they are. The children go to high school to prepare for college, and to college to prepare for a business and professional career, and they will be married sometime after graduation from college or postgraduate work. . . .

And likewise, we can often confuse these values seriously with the values of the gospel we preach. I know of a Christian neighborhood house director who for ten years in raising money for this program told over and over the story of the young son of an Italian bricklayer whom he had helped and encouraged to go to college and medical school and who became an outstanding physician. The Presbyterian elders applauded him and gave him a slice of their missionary budget. Now there is nothing in either the Old Testament or the New, so far as I know, that says our mission is to make professional men out of promising young children of the working class. And yet this is a theme that has appeared again and again in our missionary literature to reveal the class bias.[39]

3. *The Church in Social Action.* The third pattern referred to above commits the church to some thoroughgoing efforts to bring the Kingdom of God to the metropolitan area. It seeks a new definition of *agapē* fit for the metropolitan society. To some extent it is nonrational in its approach to human problems, because it seeks to find a language in which people of various levels of education and of traditional culture can communicate. At the same time it exalts rational analysis and foresight of consequences in understanding and dealing with metropolitan complexity which is new and strange to people. Paul Tillich writes of the *Strange* as characteristic of the metropolis and says that the church must accept the Strange and the questions implied within it. Since the Strange leads to questions and undermines familiar tradition, it serves to elevate reason into ultimate significance.

This church is called on to take leadership in the metropolitan community where: business leadership has broken down; political leadership has fallen down; old ethnic group leadership has dissolved; new Negro leadership has not yet matured.

This kind of church gives a priority to public as distinguished from private concerns. Pastors pay more attention to the processes and problems of the community than to the personal emotional problems of their parishioners. Religious educators balance a concern over the child's religious development with a zeal for teaching children and adults to understand and work effectively in the metropolitan community. Lay leaders of this church look for ways to give their church impact on the community's problems, rather than for ways of organizing the church for smooth internal working.

Gibson Winter sees the task of the church as nothing less than the reorganization of American urban society, and he sees this brought about through a ministry of the church in which the laymen become educated to the task and then take it as *their* task.

The reorganization of American society is some of the unfinished business of our domestic world; this is a task which we Americans have thus far avoided. The metropolitan expansion and the change in the character of American communities make it impossible to forego this responsibility any longer. . . . One further aspect of this communal situation illuminates the direction in which the reorganizing task of the laity will have to move. The breakdown of the ethnic communities leaves the urban areas with the unfinished business which they were beginning to face in the first half of the nineteenth century. We can no longer postpone the organization of a metropolitan society in which human values are respected and cultural achievements find their true place. However, the sphere of public responsibility has also been impoverished by the dissolution of ethnic ties. The ethnic communities exercised a steady pressure upon the public sphere according to their particular stage of development in American life. If one looks back upon the political formations of our great cities, it is clear that these ethnic communities have taken their turn in guiding the course of urban development as they reached the second and third generation of their tenure. Now a gap in public responsibility emerges from the breakdown of ethnic identities. Unstable urban communities provide little direct pressure on their so-called representatives and in turn exact very little recognition from the higher echelons of the metropolitan bureaucracy. Meanwhile middle-class leadership has taken flight into small-town politics in the suburban communities, leaving the metropolitan center to its own devices. The Negro ethnics are beginning to take some responsibility for central city politics, but the wealthier segments of the metropolitan community have withdrawn support and leadership from the orbit of city politics. At the very moment when our large cities face the task of urban organization, financial resources and personal leadership have been withdrawn. . . .

The Church faces several fronts on which communication needs to be opened and interpersonal community realized. The churches are quite aware that they have been relatively ineffective in the task of racial desegregation. The servanthood of the laity calls for a reflective, planned, long-range program for the racial integration of our metropolitan areas. The same applies to the social class barriers that are steadily growing in our cities; indeed, the opening of communication across social class lines may prove even more difficult than overcoming ethnic tensions between Negro and white. This task of reconciliation can be accomplished only through the planning and development of politically responsible local communities throughout the metropolitan area. Hence, the community of the servant Church has to be seriously engaged in the struggle for local community, and yet it has to be organized as a fellowship which finds its true citizenship in metropolis. The ministry of reconciliation has, therefore, the task of stabilizing local communities as open communities rather than ghettoes, and yet helping the members of these local communities to discover their true identity as citizens of metropolis. The local church as confessional assembly, preoccupied with the cultivation and nurture of its own membership, misses the real thrust of this embodiment of the New Mankind. The true pastorate is a ministry of the laity *in* the secular world; it mediates the power and vision of the New Mankind in the disrupted process of metropolitan communication.[40]

The religious leaders who are urging church activity in metropolitan renewal make use of the early Christian concept of the church member as an apostle of the Kingdom of God. " The apostolate of the laity " is a term frequently heard. Laymen must become apostles with a message for the remaking of the metropolitan community. They must feel a responsibility to God for fashioning this world as a closer approach to the Kingdom of God. They work *with* the clergy in this task, and not under the *direction* of the clergy. A Roman Catholic writer goes so far as to discard the phrase " apostolate of the laity " and replaces it by " apostolate of the church," [41] arguing that the clergy and the laymen together make up the apostolate.

Thus the emphasis is upon cooperative study and education rather than on the receiving of theological dogma by untutored laymen from tutored clergy. The church's task in the remaking of metropolis is one of self-education followed by social action.

Thoughtful people who read the contemporary exhortations to social action may remind us that the church has always wrestled with the social problems of its day — at least this has been done by the kind of church which has been dominant in Western countries. Some religious people become discouraged and conclude that there is no chance to bring the Kingdom of God to this earth. The Christian church tried it during the medieval precapitalistic period. When this kind of society broke down, the Reformation developed an active, individualistic, semireligious zeal that made some improvements in the material standard of living of the West but left unresolved some basic problems of social justice. What probability is there that the church can succeed when it has failed in the past?

The answer is that the church has an obligation to work within history for the betterment of the human condition—this is one of its solemn religious obligations. No matter what the outcome may be, this is a task of the church. This view was stated clearly by Ernst Troeltsch. He wrote in the early years of this century, before the present metropolitan problem had taken shape, but as a social historian, he could foresee some of the trends.

If the present social situation is to be controlled by Christian principles, thoughts will be necessary which have not yet been thought, and which will correspond to this new situation as the older forms met the need of the social situation in earlier ages. These ideas will have to be evolved out of the inner impulse of Christian thought, and out of its vital expression at the present time, and not exclusively out of the New Testament, in precisely the same way as both those great main types of Christian-Social philosophy were evolved out of the Christian thought of their own day, and not solely from the New Testament. And when they have been created and expressed, they will meet the fate which always awaits every fresh creation of religious and ethical thought: they will render indispensable services and they will develop profound energies, but they will never fully realize their actual ideal intention within the sphere of our earthly struggle and conflict.

As little as any other power in this world will they create the Kingdom of God upon earth as a completed social ethical organism. One of the most serious and important truths which emerge as a result of this inquiry is this: every idea is still faced by brutal facts, and all upward movement is checked and hindered by interior and exterior difficulties. Nowhere does there exist an absolute Christian ethic, which only awaits discovery; all that we can do is to learn to control the world-situation in its successive phases just as the earlier Christian ethic did in its own way. There is also no absolute ethical transformation of material nature or of human nature; all that does exist is a constant wrestling with the problems which they raise. Thus the Christian ethic of the present day and of the future will also be an adjustment to the world-situation, and it will only desire to achieve that which is practically possible. This is the cause of that ceaseless tension which drives man onward yet gives him the sense that he can never realize his ethical ideal. Only doctrinaire idealists or religious fanatics can fail to recognize these facts. Faith is the source of energy in the struggle of life, but life still remains a battle which is continually renewed upon ever new fronts. For every threatening abyss which is closed, another yawning gulf appears. The truth is — and this is the conclusion of the whole matter — the Kingdom of God is within us. But we must let our light shine before men in confident and untiring labour that they may see our good works and praise our Father in Heaven. The final ends of all humanity are hidden within His Hands.[42]

Types of Effective Churches in the Metropolitan Area

In the present situation, it has been seen that churches are subject to economic and racial stratification and segregation because of the forces of social tradition, and because the metropolitan area has a pattern of living and working arrangements that tend to force people into segregated living. However, there are three types of churches that are working realistically for improvement of this situation.

1. *The Mixed-Class and Mixed-Race Church.* In areas of the metropolis where well-to-do and poor people live, or upper-middle class and working-class people live, a church may deliberately try to combine these groups into its parish or its membership. Also, where there are Negroes or Orientals as well as whites in the local community the church can work toward a multiracial congregation. This is easier for a Roman Catholic church with a territorial parish than it is for Protestant or Jewish churches with their more limited social class and ethnic ranges. In the northern cities some middle-class churches are overcoming the race barrier by recruiting middle-class Negroes and Orientals. It appears that

the mixed-race church may be more easily attainable in northern cities than the mixed-class church.

2. *The Inner-City Church.* At a certain point in its history the Washington Square Dutch Reformed Church in New York voted to disband, " owing to the moving away of the class of population in this quarter whose needs are met by such a church." This was in 1876, and the process has been repeated many, many times since then by churches that found their " natural " clientele to be disappearing. Sometimes the church building is torn down as a part of " urban renewal." Sometimes the building is sold to a new religious group. But, in recent times, there has been an effort to maintain this kind of church as a means of serving the new population, which often is too poor and too poorly organized to create and maintain its own church.

An inner-city church is defined as one that is located in a slum area which was formerly a " better " area and from which its former members have all or nearly all moved away. (It is not a church located in the center of the city and serving transients as well as a loyal middle-class congregation who may live in apartments nearby or may live some distance away but enjoy the more cosmopolitan atmosphere of such a church. This type of church is itself an important phenomenon of metropolitan life, and belongs in the third category which will be described later.)

Often an inner-city church is maintained financially by a Protestant denomination as a missionary activity. Sometimes several Protestant denominations will cooperate to support such a church in an area from which they have withdrawn their own churches.

In addition to the good this kind of church does for the people whom it serves, who are generally needy in social and religious as well as economic terms, it may serve as a means of service by churches and church members who are located in local communities that do not have serious local social problems. Youth groups from such churches can observe the inner-city church, and can associate with youth of the inner-city church in joint service projects. Adults from the stable middle-class churches can give some of their time to the inner-city church, and can study some of the metropolitan problems in this connection.

3. *The Social Action Church.* The great majority of metropolitan area churches are physically located so that they serve one racial group and a limited social class range. In other words, their congregation is more homogeneous than the metropolitan area. This is more true of Protestant and of Jewish churches than it is of Roman Catholic churches. How can these churches act to help solve the socioethical problems of the metropolis?

This kind of church generally has a good deal of *communal* social activity. It is a fellowship, and it serves its members in their personal lives through this fellowship. Much of its value lies in its communal fellowship activity. Somehow this kind of church should combine *communal fellowship activities* with *community social action.*

The community social action should do the following things:

a. Make a thorough study of the metropolitan area, with analysis of its problems and proposed solutions for the future.

b. Engage as many adults as possible in the community study and action.

c. Teach the children and youth to study and serve the metropolitan community.

Nearly all church denominations have at least a skeleton organization for this purpose. They may have a National Federation for Social Action; they may have a Department of the Urban Church; the metropolitan area Church Federation may have one or more staff members who work in this area in the churches in the community.

The organization of Catholic Action is an example both of accomplishment and of possibility. Founded in 1934 under Pope Pius XI, it was aimed at effecting a wide participation of the laity in the life of the church. The phrase applied to its work was "apostolate of Catholic Action." The organization known as the Confraternity of Christian Doctrine publishes the magazine *Catholic Action,* and carries on an educational program. A variety of study and social action groups are found in urban Catholic parishes.

The Educational Program of the Social Action Church

The church of social action consciously and explicitly assumes responsibility for helping to raise the quality of life in the entire metropolitan area. It works for ethical goals of metropolitan development and urban renewal.

Through its educational program this church seeks to develop a religious mind and personality fit for this half of the twentieth century. This is essentially a rational, foresightful, active, and ethical mind. It is not Catholic, Jewish, Protestant; not Negro, not white.

Such people are a nuclear group in any given local church. They make up the local social action committee. Their numbers can be increased by a slow and steady adult education program. The educational program of this church uses both intellectual or cognitive methods and affective methods.

The intellectual methods are employed in study groups, discussions, and formulation of policies of social action for the local church. Such matters as the following will be studied: population changes in the local metropolitan area; problems of metropolitan government; urban renewal programs and projects; racial integration in the public and church schools.

The affective methods are employed in action groups. Through working in action groups within the church and in cooperation with other churches, individuals learn to communicate with people of other social classes and other races. A kind of volunteer metropolitan peace corps can be organized by the churches.

Education for brotherhood in the metropolitan community must be education of and for adults, first and foremost. There is much to be learned and worked out by adults before a program for children and youth can be set up in any detail. But the participation of youth in social action is essential and cannot be delayed, once the outlines of desirable social action have been traced out by the adults.

V. THE CHURCH AND WORLD BROTHERHOOD: WHAT AND HOW TO TEACH

" Go therefore, and make disciples of all nations . . . , teaching them to observe all things that I have commanded you; and lo, I am with you always, to the close of the age." This last command of Jesus' has been interpreted in our times to mean that Christians should carry the valuable things of their culture to people who lack these things. To serve the whole world in a spirit of brotherhood is one of the noblest activities of the church, and one that the youngest member as well as the oldest can understand. Every time an offering is given for missions, the people get a lesson in world brotherhood. Every time a returned missionary tells his story to a local congregation, the members have an experience of what it means to serve their fellowman.

Missions and World Brotherhood

Bringing health, the power to read, better farming methods, and methods of making community life more satisfactory, the modern missionary practices world brotherhood, and we all become better people by supporting him. Foreign missions are a counterpart to the church's mission to megalopolis. To *work* for the Kingdom of God on earth is an educative experience that does not require much involved or abstract reasoning. The simplest person can understand it.

From a young American teaching at an Indian college comes the following account of a work-camp experience. " We were building a chapel and leveling ground for the first classroom building of the —— Church Industrial Training Center. One morning we suddenly heard that someone had been hurt. In the distance we could see someone being carried down the hill. A Methodist girl from Malaya said, 'I hope it was not one of us.' We were struck by the inclusiveness of her 'us.' She did not mean only one of 'us' Methodists. As we worked for a common cause we were one whether we were Methodists or Kananaya Syrian Orthodox or Salvation Army. The 'us' included not only Malayan students, but students, teachers, and young professional people from seven other countries and most of the states of India. We had bridged the international tension between India and Pakistan, Indonesia and Malaya, East and West." This kind of experience can have a powerful effect on young people, and all kinds of people can read about it with empathy.

Learning about the practice of brotherhood in any part of the world is a form of religious education, just as the practice of brotherhood is the practice of religion. The study of brotherhood extending across national boundaries might well have a large part in every church education program. There is hardly anything more important in the religious education of American church members than the period of examination and redirection of Christian missions through which a number of denominations passed some forty years ago.

Anyplace in the world that needs assistance with problems of poverty, disease, and economic and social apathy is a place where Christians can express *agapē*. The writer has observed missionary work in Brazil, where he has traveled widely in recent years. He has felt surer of his approval for the various missionary activities than he has of his approval for some of the United States Government programs of foreign aid.

Brazil is a vast country with extremes of backwardness and of modernism, of poverty and of wealth. Her average per capita income is about one eighth of the per capita income of the U.S.A. Although the Brazilian Catholic and Protestant and Jewish churches are working for the betterment of their people, they feel an almost overpowering pressure of need, and they welcome missionaries from abroad. The good done by the missionaries is matched by the good received by their North American supporters who thus serve the Kingdom of God. The writer observed the following variety of missionary activities.

Catalão is the county seat of a county with a population of twenty-six thousand in the state of Goiás, on the midwestern frontier of Brazil. This is an old and stagnating frontier, with its first settlement going back at least a century and a half. The countryside is fair and rolling, with fields of sugarcane and pasture for cattle. Living on the large fazendas or plantations are many families of farm laborers whose grandparents worked the same land as slaves, ninety years ago. The town reflects the economic and cultural apathy of the region. There is only one small secondary school. This school was established a few years ago by an order of North American Catholic priests. They provide the only chance for youth to get past bare literacy to a position with a fair income in local business, and for a few young people each year to go to a university.

Leopoldina is a county seat of eighteen thousand people, in hilly country in the state of Minas Gerais. It has been supported by brick works and a few small factories for a century, and is the center of a general farming area. The schools are as good as average, but still only about 50 percent of the children get past the first grade, because so many of them do not master the art of reading. Here a mission of several young North American women is working with the schoolteachers to improve the teaching of reading. The Americans are sent out by a fundamentalist denomination, with the aim of teaching people to study the Bible. They are trained in techniques of linguistic analysis, and are studying the local Portuguese dialect and the local vocabulary with a tape recorder to obtain examples of local speech from parents. They expect to produce a set of readers, using familiar words of the local vocabulary. These are the words children use and hear, and the readers based on them may increase substantially the reading ability of children of the lower social class.

Uruguaiana is a city of fifty thousand on the Uruguay River, which forms the boundary between Brazil and Argentina in the southwest of the Brazilian state of Rio Grande do Sul. It is a center for rice culture and also for the business dealings of vast cattle and sheep ranches that surround the town. There are two young Mormon missionaries working in Uruguaiana, building up a local church on Mormon principles of brotherhood and community service. These young men help people to learn to work together for the common good.

In one of the slum areas of Rio de Janeiro is the Methodist People's Institute. Partially staffed and supported by North American Methodists, the Institute offers family and medical services as well as religious services, and helps the poor people to organize their local slum areas for better community living.

The Peace Corps is a contribution to world brotherhood closely enough linked to modern missions to deserve the moral support of the churches, and to become a subject of education and study in the church. If some form of world and domestic service corps grows out of the Peace Corps, the churches may well cooperate with such a program as far as the principle of separation of church and state permits.

One World and the Church

The mass of mankind is striving in a halting way to reduce international conflict and tension and to produce a peaceful, stable world in which the nations can cooperate for human welfare. There are some who hope and plan for the unification of mankind in one single society. They believe that this society should have a political, economic, and ethical unity. It would become an ecumenical state, diverting its resources from warfare and economic competition into service for the welfare of human beings. UNESCO exists with the task of promoting international cooperation and understanding on an intellectual and cultural plane. In 1956, UNESCO established a ten-year Major Project devoted to "Mutual Appreciation of Eastern and Western Cultural Values." The work of UNESCO in this project is devoted to finding a basis for harmonious coexistence and a limited degree of cooperation. UNESCO has avoided what might be called explicit interreligious relations, probably because its leaders felt that religion was more a divisive than a unitive force among the various parts of the world.

Since world peace and world order are desired by all the great living religions, it would seem that the United Nations, UNESCO, and the other intergovernmental organizations should be the subject of friendly interest, study, and support by the religious bodies of the world. The religious bodies should instruct their members at least in the sociological explanations of the trend toward interdependence of nations and world unity.

Every great religion can probably go farther, and teach its own view of the moral and religious bases for world unity. There is even some justification for believing that the unification of mankind is more likely to come through one world religion than through one world government. The church must decide for itself:

1. What to do and to teach about world unity.
2. Whether a world religion is a possibility, and, if so, whether it is desirable.

Arnold Toynbee is perhaps the most widely read proponent not only of world unity but also of a world religion. He writes, "The annihilation of distance through the achievements of a Late Modern Western technology has brought all the living higher religions all over the world into a much closer contact with one another than before." The arguments in favor of a world religion are important, and need to be considered and discussed by every church that is interested in world brotherhood. This should be a part of the educational program of every such church.

Perhaps, though, the question first to be studied is, What contribution can religion make in the field of international relations? This question can be answered by a particular church with words about world brotherhood, but there is a catch in such an answer, as Hendrik Kraemer has pointed out.

> Everybody knows that this evasive entity called religion in the singular gets in fact its tangible meaning, especially in the sphere of relationship and understanding, only within each of the many existing religions. Religion in the singular is easily extolled or recommended as a bond, or cement, of unity. This kind of thinking and pleading is in our days much in vogue, but in practice it is, except

for the reality-proof idealists, evident that problems like world peace and world stability are not yielding to noble wishful thinking. When religion in the singular is called upon to serve the great pragmatic ends of world peace and world stability, because of its depth and loftiness, the religions in the plural come immediately on the scene and have to define their possible common contribution to the service required. The disappointing experience then often follows that no intellectually construed universal religion, comprising all the necessary attributes for the unification of all minds, appears able to remove the fact that the concrete religions are more steeped in their peculiar habitus and consciousness than in these wishful fictions. It is, therefore, a recurrent fact that in meetings devoted to the search for unity and harmony in our sadly divided world, voices are heard saying that religion is a divisive and not a unitive influence. Therefore better no religion at all than one that is fanatical and intolerant. The fact of this alleged divisive influence of religion(s), in relation to each other or even within the same religious body, is patent enough all over the world.

This single point deserves specific notice, because it shows that the predicament in which the world today finds itself, the understandable longing for peace and harmony, are powerful instigations towards testing and evaluating the capacity of religion and religions for bringing men together instead of disuniting them, and for producing tolerance and forbearance. Not in theory, but in practice. It is indubitable that tolerance, creating unity, and the will towards mutual understanding, are very important tests as at present applied to religion as a viable power. The oft-recurring practical deficiency in this respect brings religion into disrepute. Particularly as the humanitarian principles of human solidarity and responsibility for one's neighbour not only have a universal appeal, just because they are " de-religionized," but also are often more effective than religious injunctions. Frequently such religious injunctions, although they are in fact of the same high moral calibre as the humanitarian ones and often even profounder, become somehow morally inoperative because some element of religious bigotry creeps in.[43]

A World Religion?

In a fascinating novel entitled *Round the Bend,*[44] the Australian writer, Nevil Shute, imagines the second coming of the Messiah in this century. His protagonist is the son of a mixed Oriental-

Caucasian marriage, who gets an ordinary education in Malaya and London, and goes to work as an aviation mechanic at airfields in the British Commonwealth, changing jobs frequently. A striking thing about the young man is his intense interest in the religion of any land where he happens to be. He talks about religion to his workmates, and before long he has a group of devoted disciples wherever he is, in India, the Near East, the Far East. They create a kind of universal ethics for a technological era, and this gives meaning to their work. The young man is especially close to Buddhists but he also gets along well with Muslim priests. He appears to be working out a coherent set of religious concepts that are good for any place and culture in the contemporary world that is becoming bound together by technology. But at the age of about thirty-three he sickens and dies, leaving behind a band of followers who are full of enthusiasm but not clear just what their mission is. Toward the close of his life he is offered a fortune by a wealthy Arab sheikh for the spreading of his words, and he declines it, saying: "My teaching has no need of temples. My temples are the fitters' shop, the toolroom, and the hangar on the aerodrome. Nor do I need priests for what I teach, because each man who finds God in his daily work by working in a shop with other men, he is a priest for me. . . . Men who follow my teaching become good workmen, because good work and right thinking are as one." His legend spreads, and pilgrims come to see him as the news spreads that he is dying. His sister says, during his last illness, "These people that come here to see him — they think he's a man, but a man touched by the hand of God, whichever form of God they happen to believe in."

Great religious movements have started in the past through the life of one man, and they may do so again through the emergence of a single world leader. But the question of the possibility of the development of a single world religion is more usefully considered as one for the present living religions to answer. Can they unite in a world religion? For the consideration of this question in this essay, we shall present the argument of the historian Toynbee, and the counterargument of Hendrik

Kraemer, the student of comparative religion.

Toynbee argues that the great faiths which have held sway in one or another part of the world have in them a common universally valid essence, which is adapted to the time and place in which they exist sociologically. Every religion develops its own distinct orientation toward the various aspects of life. These orientations are now merging for many groups, making it possible to speak of a world religion.

The great religions grew up generally in separate parts of the world, or at widely separate times, in response to a social situation that called for a new wave of religious feeling. Each arose in a period of disillusionment with the world and hope for salvation. The old religious answers would not do. But nevertheless there was continuity with the old religions and with others to come in other places. Toynbee sees the seven great living religions having the same essential truths:

1. The universe is mysterious — men do not understand it all.
2. There is a Presence in the universe greater than man himself.
3. Absolute Reality has a personal aspect — God. (The only world religion to deny this is Hinayana Buddhism.)
4. Man's goal is to seek communion with the presence behind phenomena.
5. The human self must get rid of its innate self-centeredness.
6. Knowledge is not an end in itself, but a means to action.

These are characteristic (with the exception noted) of: Judaism; Christianity; Islam; Zoroastrianism; the Hinayana Buddhism of Ceylon and Southeast Asia; the Mahayana Buddhism of Tibet, Mongolia, and East Asia; and the post-Buddhist Hinduism of India.

Religion is always being translated into the language of a particular social milieu, and adapted to the needs of a given time and place in history. Every religion receives accidental accretions from the cultures into which it spreads. Thus, Christianity received Anglo-Saxon and Greco-Roman rites during its early centuries. In Brazil, the African slaves influenced the forms of Christian worship. In northern Mexico there is a religious movement known as the Sonora Catholic Church created by Indians and combining some of their indigenous religious practices with others they have taken from the Roman Catholic Church.

> These accidental accretions are the price that the permanently and universally valid essence of a higher religion has to pay for communicating its message to the members of a particular society in a particular stage of this society's history. . . . The message has to be denatured to some extent by a translation of what is permanent and universal into terms of something that is temporary and local.[45]

These "accidental accretions" should be peeled off of phenomenal religion, in order to develop a form of world religion in a period of world unity. Some of them are:

1. Holy places
2. Rituals
3. Taboos
4. Social conventions with a religious backing, such as a particular form of marriage.
5. Myths—such as the virgin birth, and the sacrifice of life by a Savior.
6. Theology—"The price a religion pays for the conversion of intellectuals."
7. Self-centeredness—the belief that one's own form is the only true religion.

One has only to read this list to see that most people are hardly ready for a world religion on Toynbee's terms. Some people would ask what there is left after the "peeling away" of the items listed. The answer is that there would be a very abstract common essence, consisting of such propositions as the following:

The universe is a society of selves.

True religion is the practice of love or service to other selves.

All forms of religion have some truth.

But around this essence would be built new concrete teachings that fit the world culture which is coming into being. New myths and images would have to be created to carry the meanings for action of the world religion. For example, such novels as that of Nevil Shute might become read as religious literature.

Other Western scholars of culture and religion have also agreed upon the desirability and possibility of a world religion. Hocking sees all religions as essentially one. He believes that the essence of Christianity is one with the essence of other religions, and that a rethinking of Christianity can make it an acceptable basis for a world religion in a world civilization. The philosopher F. C. S. Northrop sees the coming of a unified philosophy combining the philosophical approaches of East and West and leading to world understanding, though this might not be recognized as having a religious basis.

Over against these spokesmen for an emerging world religion stands Hendrik Kraemer. He believes that Toynbee is not " religious " enough to support the truly important elements of Christianity. He fears that " world peace planners and world improvers, who are in religious respects rather indifferent, try to *use* religion and religions as reservoirs of resources and tools " for the creation of world unity. Kraemer writes:

Arnold Toynbee, both in his Gifford Lectures and in his *Christianity Among the Religions of the World,* notwithstanding his subjective faithfulness to the " Christian " tradition and his use of Christian terms, reveals in his fundamental position exactly the Indian or East-Asian pragmatist attitude towards religion. In principle he can walk, like an Asian sage, all ways, but in practice for convenience's sake he prefers the accustomed " Christian " way, certainly also for reasons of genuine affection. His whole trend of expressing himself suggests an intellectual preference for the Asian conception of religion. As he is seriously concerned about good inter-religious relationships as a new issue and cultural task, he speaks repeatedly about the qualifications of the different great religions for good-neighbourship. In this respect there is in his opinion no trouble from the side of the higher religions of East Asia. By their innate tolerance they are admirably fitted for the " job." The trouble lies with Christianity, Judaism and Islam. . . .

He reflects in his representations widespread, modern religious feeling, which spontaneously rejects all that suggests exclusiveness, intolerance or the thesis of the uniqueness of Christianity. At the same time he is one of the main feeders of this attitude. The more so because Toynbee's way of reasoning, led by a simplistic rationalism and emotionalism in one, has an easy appeal to modern religious feeling. In our context the main point, however, is that his method of equating and differentiating the religions is only understandable in Hindu perspective. Nor is it less important that the appeal it makes is an indication of the fact that the Indian pragmatic view of religion, although still motivated under typically Christian angles of view, has penetrated far more deeply into many minds in the West than is generally realized. Asian thinking achieves already many effortless victories in the West. Its claim to be undogmatic and tolerant chimes in with the modern mind. Panikkar quietly says that Hinduism knows its position is unassailable and that a doctrine of the monopoly of Truth and Revelation is absurd to the Asian mind.[46]

Kraemer equates Toynbee's position with that of Symmachus the pagan Roman statesman who debated with Ambrose in the fourth century, saying, "It is not possible that a mystery so great (as religious truth) should be accessible by one road alone." But Kraemer argues that Christianity has a *revelation* which cuts through the *mystery*. Jesus Christ as the Revelation of God is at once exclusive and inclusive. What is absolute is not Christianity but the Revelation of God in Jesus Christ.[47] For Kraemer, Christ is the Absolute Truth, and the source of revelation. This sets Christianity off from other religions and makes them basically incompatible.

The question is whether the various great religions can find compatibility in a single world religion. Can they recognize and grant to other religions the validity for other parts of the world that they claim for their own areas? Can they teach their members that their version of religious truth is only one of several valid versions?

There are two alternatives for religious people who are sincerely working for world brotherhood:

1. A single unified world religion, combining the common elements of all modern religions. There would be local variations related to such cultural realities as social class, ethnic traditions, and perhaps personality types among people.

2. A continuous dialogue between religions in the mood of understanding, but not at the cost of seeking compromise above

everything else. It would be based on a seriousness about religion and a feeling of responsibility for cooperation and a sense of the need for building a new world of mutual understanding.

Kraemer favors the second of these alternatives. He believes that the great living religions should keep themselves apart but try to learn from one another. The spiritual life of man must find new forms of expression in all religions. For all major religions the paramount problems are the same. "We should steep ourselves in one another's problems and be ready to serve one another in word and deed." He looks forward to a Great Dialogue between the world's religions.

The central issue in this coming dialogue with the grand, elusive Eastern systems of *humanist* thinking will, it seems, be to vindicate the *personal* conception of the living God as manifest in Jesus Christ, and the meaning and purpose of Man and the World in the light of God's self-disclosure in the historical Jesus Christ. The keyword of Oriental humanistic philosophies is Harmony. In this respect they betray again that they are impressive elaborations of the fundamental aspirations and tendencies of the universal, primitive, archaic systems of life and the world, centering around the harmony of man, nature and cosmos and glossing over the glaring disharmonies in man's inner and outer life.

This vindication in the face of, and in dialogue with, the fascinating religious philosophies of the East is a far more arduous enterprise than Christianity has ever experienced in its meeting in history with so-called classical Humanism. Classical Humanism is in comparison with Humanisms of the East a respectable but rather pale affair. The only point of comparison to be found in Church history is the renowned struggle of the Church with Gnosticism. In my opinion the coming dialogue will, if anything, most certainly imply a new dialogue and combat with Gnosticism, but in a wholly new setting. It is worth while to note that the Gnosticism of the past was of an essentially Eastern temper.

Another point of great importance in building up fruitful interreligious relationships and contacts is to make a clear distinction in aims. There may be two aims: a pragmatic or a fundamental one. The pragmatic has to aim first and foremost at removing mutual misunderstandings and serving common human responsibilities. This may lead on to a deeper exchange of witness and experience, but if so it is a by-product. The fundamental aim directly involves this open exchange of witness, experience, cross-questioning and listening. The seriousness of true religion demands that one shall be really one's religious self and avoid the temptation — and this is valid for both cases, the pragmatic and the fundamental — of putting as an indispensable condition of dialogue and relationship the assumption that all religions are essentially one. As an axiomatic assumption it robs all true religion of its seriousness. This seriousness need not hinder participants from being open to new insights through the instrumentality of contact with one another. . . .

Another way of saying the same thing is that a new apologetic of the Christian Faith is an imperative demand. In this case, of course, it should be an apologetic arising out of a sincere and open dialogue with the non-Christian religions. It is simply a parallel to the other great *apologia nova* that Christian thinkers are called to in the present situation, viz. the dialogue with the vast new thinking on the Universe and Man by modern secularity. . . . I use the term "Christian thinkers" advisedly here, because it is by no means only the theologians who are summoned, but the great number of Christian lay people who co-operate fully in the vast enterprise of theoretical and applied sciences in every field. For they are not only intellectually but existentially confronted by the demand to spell out their faith in correlation with the new adventurous realm of apprehension of world, life and man, implied in the elusive term "modern world." The meeting with the philosophies and religions of the East is part of this complex. This two-sided dialogue or *apologia* is one of the greatest issues of the Christian world. In my conviction, if it is fearlessly met on the basis of well-considered ecumenical planning it is one of the surest ways towards a real regaining of intellectual responsibility and dignity.[48]

Thus Kraemer favors cooperation of the world's religions through discussions and debates that could be fostered through ecumenical planning.

The Christian Church and other Western churches must decide what and how to teach about other religions in an interdependent world where the North American–European version of things is not *ipso facto* superior.

There will certainly be a wide variety of practices among the various churches on this matter of teaching about a world religion, as well as on the matter of teaching about world government, missionaries, and other ways of expressing and achieving brotherhood. On the one hand, the otherworldly, fundamentalist church is likely to have nationalist leanings and therefore to teach a view of the world that is mistrustful of other national governments and of other religions. It may support foreign missions as a part of its evangelical program and through missions it will probably seek to practice brotherhood. On the other hand, the liberal nontheistic churches are likely to teach positively for a world religion and to support efforts toward a world government.

Not many people really expect or desire a new worldwide syncretic religion. They are impressed by the lack of religiosity in the contemporary world. This secularism, or worldliness, or lack of religiosity is responsible both for vast accomplishments of the modern age, as well as many of its failures. Modern man tends to glorify his scientific knowledge and his technical skill, and to forget his former awareness of depending upon a force in the universe that is beyond him. Hans Morgenthau looks doubtfully at the prospect of a world syncretic religion. He thinks that such a religion is bound to lack religiosity. Religiosity has within it feelings of mystery, tragedy, and guilt, which are not likely to be part of a syncretic religion.

> The clarion calling a civilization to return to religion, en masse as it were, finds, and must find, its response in an eclectic idolatry, often blasphemous in man's self-identification with the deity, which popularizes the trappings of religion without reviving the dormant substance of its religiosity. To restore man to the fulness of his stature and thus give his civilization a new lease on life requires indeed the teaching of men like Mr. Toynbee. Yet their teaching must seek to illuminate a mysterious, tragic, and sinful experience common to all men in terms of a religiosity likewise common to all men. Neither a teacher nor a whole civilization can by an act of will create the symbolic and ritualistic expressions of religiosity thus restored; least of all can they create them out of the fragments of religions, whose decline has made the restoration of religiosity necessary in the first place.

What religions will grow from this new religiosity man must leave to fate. He must be content to be ready, and to make others ready, to see the signs and to read them aright when they appear.[49]

The Ecumenical Movement and World Brotherhood

In the vast majority of churches there is likely to be an ecumenical drift, or perhaps a more rapid motion that could hardly be called a drift. This is what Kraemer calls for — a vigorous give-and-take among the great religious bodies which challenges each one to apply its energies to the making of a better world. With the World Council of Churches gaining strength rapidly after World War II, the non-Roman Catholic Christian churches were at least partially prepared for cooperation with the Vatican Ecumenical Council convened by Pope John in 1962 for the purpose of moving the Roman Catholic Church toward Christian unity. Pope Paul called the second session of the Council in 1963, and this session completed the first three chapters of a five-chapter document on Christian unity. The Vatican Secretariat for Christian Unity seeks to improve relations between Roman Catholics and other Christians. The 1962 meeting of the National Catholic Educational Association centered around the theme "Fostering the Ecumenical Spirit." Papers were read at this meeting which favored various forms of ecumenism on the college campus.

The Catholic student can go inter-faith in a number of ways: by serving on joint boards made up of students of various religions; by working for schools of religious knowledge; by joint meetings and projects staged with members of other religious student groups; by joint discussions among students where such is permitted by the Ordinary; by promotion of joint religious projects on campus.[50]

Extension of the ecumenical movement to cover all the world religions is only a matter of time. One goal of the movement will be to teach people to understand and appreciate other religions. Another goal will be to teach the universal essentials of religious ethics as these emerge from the conversations and discussions between representatives of the several world religions. In 1964, Pope Paul VI established a Vatican Secretariat for non-Christians that has the task of maintaining relations with all the non-Christian religions.

How far can ecumenism lead? Kraemer and others would hope that it might lead to a strengthening of existing religions, but not a merging of them.

Conclusions Concerning Religious Education and World Brotherhood

What, then, should be the content of religious education in relation to world brotherhood? A church can teach about foreign missions for a simple concrete interpretation of world brotherhood. It can teach world unity as an ethical imperative for a religious solution of political and social problems and the cessation of war. It can teach for understanding of the world religions and for some version of ecumenism based on religiosity. It can encourage men to think about cooperation between the world religions.

Each new generation has a chance to begin anew to learn the essentials of religion, and this opportunity is a precious one in the contemporary world. How should religion be taught in relation to an oncoming world culture? The churches must work this out for their adults and then teach it to their children.

Perhaps the analogy may be drawn with the teaching of the "new mathematics" in the schools. There is no change in the nature of mathematical truth, but there is a major change in the methods of teaching the subject. Children are being taught the *structure* of mathematics, together with a set of computational skills. By structure of a subject we mean its underlying propositions and the connections among them.

Perhaps the teachers of religion will undertake to teach the *structure* of religion. This may be the goal of the several Protestant denominations which are working together on a curriculum for the church school under the auspices of the National Council of Churches. Where different specific religious groups get together to cooperate in thinking about curriculum, they may penetrate below their superficial differences to their basic similarities. And a similar cooperation among the great world religions might have similar value.

Another goal of an effective educational system is to teach the pupil to think and behave like the expert in the field being studied. That is, the secular school attempts to teach pupils to think and behave like scientists, or historians, or mathematicians. Can the church teach children to think and behave like experts in religion? Here the " expert " is the saint, rather than the theologian. This seems farfetched, but no more so than the idea that a ten-year-old should learn to think like Galileo or Einstein. Clearly, the child is to approach the heroes of science or of religion as ideals, and to learn from them imperfectly. Perhaps this will be possible, if the church can identify its saints and present them concretely to students. Many of the saints will be such modern people as Schweitzer and Gandhi who appear concretely to the student, and from whom he can learn more easily because he himself lives in the same period of history.

With respect to the teaching of world brotherhood, the church should use *affective* education at the first levels. With children as well as with the simple people of all ages, religion must be taught in its concreteness. It must have psychological validity for the individual person, as well as sociological validity for the group. This is where the teaching about missions and the experience of working with and sharing with people of other cultures and other faiths is important.

Teaching for world brotherhood also requires *intellective* education. The church needs to analyze the oncoming social reality of an interdependent world and to relate this to the essentials of religion, just as the school should relate the oncoming social reality to the essentials of social science.

The oncoming social reality in which world brotherhood is to be achieved has several basic *facts,* and presents several major problems. It is these facts and problems which should be analyzed, understood, and acted upon. Some of the content to be studied is religious, but much of it is secular. Whether explicitly religious or secular, this is the appropriate content for religious education:

1. The ecumenical movement in religion, and the attempt at communication and understanding among the great world religions.

2. The problems of maintaining peace and world order.

3. The peaceful service provided to human beings by national governments and international organizations.

4. The array of problems of maintaining human freedom and initiative in a world of growing order and interrelatedness.

Individuality and autonomy are ethical ideals, which may seem to be threatened by contemporary social changes. How much of individuality and autonomy must be sacrificed for desirable social goals? What about population control, control of the use and exploitation of arable land, the rights of people to an income sufficient for comfortable living, control of the applications of science? In all these areas of life, the desires of a single individual are subject to a system of social controls, and this system may be worked out on the basis of rational ethics.

This is the challenge to the curriculum of religious education—how to teach youth and adults about the oncoming reality of an interdependent world so as to bring their religiosity into a rational supporting system for beliefs and behavior leading to world brotherhood.

NOTES

1. Gerhard Lenski, *The Religious Factor* (Doubleday & Company, Inc., 1961).

2. D. Campbell Wyckoff, " The Design of Protestant Curriculum," p. 1. Presentation at the meeting of the Curriculum Study Committee, November 30 to December 4, 1959. National Council of the Churches of Christ in the U.S.A.

3. Robert J. Havighurst, *Human Development and Education* (David McKay Company, Inc., 1953), Ch. 14.

4. Horace Bushnell, *Christian Nurture* (first published in 1847; Yale University Press, 1947).

5. Wyckoff, *op. cit.*, p. 3.

6. Robert J. Havighurst and H. G. Morgan, *The Social History of a War-Boom Community* (Longmans, Green & Co., Inc., 1951), p. 160.

7. Nevitt Sanford, ed., *The American College* (John Wiley & Son, Inc., 1962), p. 90.

8. Ellen G. White, *Testimonies for the Church* (Pacific Press, 1900), Vol. 6, pp. 145–146.

9. George Hagmaier, C.S.P., " Comments," *Religious Education*, Vol. 58 (1963), pp. 145–147.

10. Andrew Greeley, *Religion and Career* (Sheed & Ward, Inc., 1963), Chs. 2;5.

11. Donald Ericson, " Religious Consequences of Public and Sectarian Schooling," *School Review*, Vol. 72 (Spring, 1964), p. 29.

12. Leslie Sargent, " Parochial School Education and Church Membership," *Religious Education*, Vol. 58 (1963), pp. 294–297.

13. David R. Hunter, " The Theology of Christian Education," *Religious Education*, Vol. 58 (1963), pp. 4–11.

14. Reprinted from an article "An Overview of Evaluation," by Elizabeth Hagen, in *Evaluation and Christian Education,* pp. 29–31, published by the National Council of the Churches of Christ in the U.S.A. Copyright 1960. Used by permission.

15. John W. C. Johnstone, "Adult Uses of Education: Fact and Forecast," *Sociological Backgrounds of Adult Education* (Center for the Study of Liberal Education, Chicago, 1964).

16. Havighurst, *Human Development and Education.*

17. Erik Erikson, *Childhood and Society* (W. W. Norton & Company, Inc., 1950).

18. Erik Erikson, *Young Man Luther* (W. W. Norton & Company, Inc., 1958).

19. Bernice L. Neugarten, "Personality Changes During the Adult Years," *Psychological Backgrounds of Adult Education* (Center for the Study of Liberal Education, Chicago, 1963).

20. *Ibid.,* p. 61.

21. Lawrence Kohlberg, "Moral Development and Identification," *Child Psychology: 1963,* Sixty-second Yearbook, Part I, National Society for the Study of Education (The University of Chicago Press, 1963), Ch. VII.

22. Lawrence Kohlberg, "The Development of Moral Character and Moral Ideology" in Martin Hoffman, ed., *Review of Research in Child Psychology* (Russell Sage Foundation, 1964).

23. Robert F. Peck and Robert J. Havighurst, *The Psychology of Character Development* (John Wiley & Son, Inc., 1960).

24. Lawrence Kohlberg, "The Developmental Approach to Moralization." Working Paper for Social Science Research Council Conference on Character Development, November, 1963.

25. Martin L. Hoffman, "Early Processes in Moral Development." Working Paper for Social Science Research Council Conference on Character Development, November, 1963.

26. Hugh Hartshorne and Mark May, *Studies in the Nature of Character,* 3 vols. (The Macmillan Company, 1930).

27. Robert J. Havighurst and Hilda Taba, *Adolescent Character and Personality* (John Wiley & Son, Inc., 1949; also, paperback, 1963).

28. Emmanuel Cardinal Suhard, *The Church Today* (Fides Publishers, 1953), p. 99.

29. Gibson Winter, *The New Creation as Metropolis* (The Macmillan Company, 1963), p. 33. Used by permission.

30. Val B. Clear, "The Urbanization of a Holiness Body," in Robert Lee, ed., *Cities and Churches* (The Westminster Press, 1962), pp. 207–217.

31. Winter, *op. cit.,* p. 134.

32. Martin H. Scharlemann, "Obedience in Challenge and Response," in Walter Kloetzli, ed., *Challenge and Response in the City* (Augustana Press, 1962), pp. 22–23.

33. Ernst Troeltsch, *The Social Teaching of the Christian Churches,* tr. by Olive Wyon, 2 vols. (George Allen & Unwin, Ltd., London, 1931), pp. 44–45.

34. Seymour Lipset, *Political Man* (Doubleday & Company, Inc., 1960), p. 108.

35. Joseph Fichter, *Social Relations in the Urban Parish* (The University of Chicago Press, 1954).

36. For the details of the development of this ratio, see Robert J. Havighurst and Bernice L. Neugarten, *Society and Education* (Allyn and Bacon, Inc., 1962), Ch. 13. This particular ratio is computed as follows:

$$\text{SER} = \frac{2(\text{Upper Middle}) + \text{Lower Middle}}{\text{Upper Lower} + 2(\text{Lower Lower})}$$

37. Truman B. Douglass, "The Job the Protestants Shirk," in Lee, *Cities and Churches,* p. 92.

38. Robert Lee, "The Organizational Dilemma in American Protestantism," in Lee, *Cities and Churches,* p. 228.

39. David W. Barry, "The Fellowship of Class," in Lee, *Cities and Churches,* pp. 281, 283.

40. Winter, *op. cit.,* pp. 118, 120–121, 123–124.

41. Elmer O'Brien, S.J., "Who Are the Laity?" *Unity* (November, 1963). Published by Benedict Labre House, Montreal, Canada.

42. Troeltsch, *op. cit.,* pp. 1012–1013.

43. Hendrik Kraemer, *World Cultures and World Religions: The Coming Dialogue* (The Westminster Press, 1962), pp. 351–352.

44. Nevil Shute, *Round the Bend* (William Morrow and Company, Inc., 1951), pp. 320, 334.

45. Arnold Toynbee, *An Historian's Approach to Religion* (Oxford University Press, London, 1956), p. 266.

46. Kraemer, *World Cultures and World Religions,* pp. 328, 329–330.

47. Hendrik Kraemer, *Why Christianity of All Religions?* tr. by Hubert Hoskins (The Westminster Press, 1962), pp. 104, 116.

48. Kraemer, *World Cultures and World Religions,* pp. 23, 356, 365–366.

49. Hans Morgenthau, *The Restoration of American Politics* (The University of Chicago Press, 1962), pp. 60–62.

50. George Garrelts, "Newman Clubs and Ecumenism on the Secular Campus," *National Catholic Educational Association Bulletin,* Vol. 59 (August, 1962), pp. 181–184.

INDEX